modern
rainbow
patchwork
quilts

**14 vibrant projects suitable for beginners,
plus handy techniques, tips and tricks**

modern

rainbow

patchwork

quilts

14 vibrant projects suitable for beginners,
plus handy techniques, tips and tricks

PAULA STEEL

Photographs by Jesse Wild

White Owl

I would like to dedicate this book to my husband James. This book, or indeed my quilting journey, would not have happened without you. Thank you for being so supportive and lending me some self-belief when I needed it most. A small dedication cannot express how much I love you; thank you for loving me back and valuing my happiness. I also need to say thank you to my daughter Ella, who helped by making cups of tea and trimming a few blocks, when bribed. I love you; now go and make some space in your room for a few more quilts!

First published in Great Britain in 2020 by
PEN & SWORD WHITE OWL
An imprint of Pen & Sword Books Ltd
Yorkshire – Philadelphia

Copyright © Paula Steel, 2020

ISBN 9781526752413

The right of Paula Steel to be identified as Author of this work has been asserted by her in accordance with the Copyright, Designs and Patents Act 1988.
A CIP catalogue record for this book is available from the British Library.

Group Publisher: Jonathan Wright
Series Editor and Publishing Consultant: Katherine Raderecht
Photography: Jesse Wild
Art Director: Jane Toft
Copy Editor: Katherine Raderecht
Stylist: Jaine Bevan

Printed and bound in India, by Replika Press Pvt. Ltd.

Pen & Sword Books Ltd incorporates the Imprints of Pen & Sword Books
Archaeology, Atlas, Aviation, Battleground, Discovery, Family History, History, Maritime, Military, Naval, Politics, Railways, Select, Transport, True Crime, Fiction, Frontline Books, Leo Cooper, Praetorian Press, Seaforth Publishing, Wharncliffe and White Owl.

For a complete list of Pen & Sword titles please contact:

PEN & SWORD BOOKS LIMITED
47 Church Street, Barnsley, South Yorkshire S70 2AS, England
E-mail: enquiries@pen-and-sword.co.uk
Website: www.pen-and-sword.co.uk
or
PEN AND SWORD BOOKS
1950 Lawrence Rd, Havertown, PA 19083, USA
E-mail: Uspen-and-sword@casematepublishers.com
Website: www.penandswordbooks.com

contents

introduction

Who am I? I'm Paula Steel and I have been sewing and quilting for over six years now. That might sound like an introduction to a self-help group but there's no way I will give up my quilting addiction. I happily inherited a creative flair from my Grandma Audrey, with a love of logic and general maths nerdiness passed down from my Dad.

I first found quilting after initially attempting dressmaking, falling in love with the combination of creativity, colour and quilt maths. I spend most of my time as a quilting technical editor, designing and writing patterns for quilt magazines, and sewing for fun in my spare time of course. I work in my lovely sewing room at home in Lancashire with the help of my two feline assistants Maggie and Indy, who aren't always too helpful.

So why rainbows? Well, I am heavily influenced by my late 80s/early 90s childhood: think Care Bears, Rainbow Brite and Lego. Rainbows made me feel warm and fuzzy back then and they still do! It's not just about fabric either - show me pretty much anything lined up in Rainbow order and the little colour magpie within me gets all excited. The projects in this book cover bright rainbows, plus my take on a more grown up muted rainbow and an 80s neon rainbow.

Who is the book for? It is suitable for beginners as well as more confident quilters and there are plenty of tutorials covering all of the necessary skills needed. There were lots of quilting books that inspired me when I started my quilting adventure and I hope you will find some inspiration in this one. If you are a beginner then take your time and practise. Don't be afraid of making mistakes - I still make plenty of them. Have fun, be proud of what you achieve and enjoy the learning.

You can download the quilt templates from:
www.pen-and-sword.co.uk/Modern-Rainbow-Patchwork-Quilts-Paperback/p/17128

chapter one: the basics

Let's start with the basics. This section offers an insight into the different types of fabric available and tips on creating a rainbow that is right for you. For beginners, I've included some quilting basics and a list of the tools you'll need...

USING COLOUR AND FABRIC OPTIONS
Rainbow order (ROYGBIV)

If you went to school in the UK, you might know the little ditty:

Richard **O**f **Y**ork **G**ave **B**attle **I**n **V**ain.

Red, **O**range, **Y**ellow, **G**reen, **B**lue, **I**ndigo (or Purple), **V**iolet (or Pink)

That's how I remember my order, but you don't need to be completely prescriptive. Leave out a purple and throw in some more pink shades? It still has that rainbow vibe.

Use the whole rainbow, or choose part of it?

For our rainbow projects we are mainly concentrating on the rainbow aesthetic, i.e. all of the colours together, but sometimes you may need more than seven. This is where the colour wheel comes in. Simply add a mid-colour in between the main seven colours. A few of the designs use eight colours so just add in your favourite mid-colour. I'm a big fan of blue-green.

Patterned Your rainbow projects don't need to be plain and there are some fantastic patterned prints out there. For the rainbow projects you are mainly looking for fabrics that have an obvious dominant colour. This will give you the definition required.

Low Volume I'm a big fan of using plain white as a background because it can really make colours pop, but it isn't to everyone's taste. This is where low volume prints come in. They are mainly white/cream with some printed text or geometric designs. Low volume can range from almost completely white to being monotone. Using these fabrics adds depth and interest to your quilt's background. I've also used some low volume fabrics that are white with one other colour. The Vintage Star quilt uses these fabrics and I love the scrappy feel it gives.

Blenders Blenders are tone on tone fabrics where fabrics have patterns in slightly different shades of one colour. Blenders work really well for the rainbow projects as they read very strongly as one colour but have a little bit of extra interest.

Solid/plain colours Solids are one of my favourite fabrics to work with. There is such a huge variety available, making it easy to get the colours you need. I really enjoy using solids to create patterns. I think it's a bit like making Lego houses, which reminds me of my childhood!

Patterned

Low Volume

Solid / Plain colours

SOURCING YOUR FABRICS, FINDING A RAINBOW

There are lots of lovely places to buy fabrics and you can see a list of my favourites on page 111. If you are looking to increase your stash of rainbow suitable fabrics, then I would suggest you first organise your fabric stash into colour order. You will probably find that you have lots of one or two colours but not as much of the others. Me? I always seem to have lots of blue/ green fabrics but very little purple.

USEFUL TOOLS / THINGS YOU WILL NEED

It's easy to fill up your sewing space, cupboards and counters with numerous sewing notions and useful knick-knacks. I'm fond of new exciting tools, not to mention my over populated pen pots! So, to try and help, I've put together a list of the simple essentials you will need. I have also put a little list of the extras at the bottom. If, like me, you can't help but try something new, have a little look at what I like to use.

Fabric Requirements	Rounded up in cm	Buying amount
Fat Quarter	Fat Quarter	Fat Quarter
¼ Yd (9" x WOF)	23cm	¼ m
⅓ yd (12" x WOF)	31cm	½ m
½ Yd (18" x WOF)	46cm	½ m
⅔ Yd (24" x WOF)	61cm	¾ m
¾ Yd – (27" x WOF)	69cm	¾ m
1 Yd – (36" x WOF)	92cm	1m
1 ¼ Yds (45" x WOF)	15cm	1 ¼ m
1 ⅓ yds (48" x WOF)	122cm	1 ¼ m
1 ½ Yds (54" x WOF)	138cm	1 ½ m
1 ⅔ Yds (60" x WOF)	52cm	1 ¾ m
1 ¾ Yds – (63" x WOF)	161cm	1 ¾ m
2 Yds (72" x WOF)	183cm	2m
3 Yds (108" x WOF)	275cm	2 ¾ m
4 Yds (144" x WOF)	366cm	3 ¾ m
5 Yds (180" x WOF)	458cm	4 ¾ m

Remember: 1 yard is 36" and to calculate centimetres from inches multiply by 2.54.

A selection of my must-have tools and my nice-to-have extras, like the wonderfully scented Flatter spray

ESSENTIALS

The obvious – First things first. You will obviously need a sewing machine, some thread, pins, binding clips, hand sewing needles and some scissors. Fabric too, of course - more about that in the colour section!

Rotary Cutter – I use a 45mm rotary cutter, which works well. They also come in smaller or larger sizes. Do be careful with them, they are very sharp. Get in the habit of closing them once you have finished cutting, your fingers will thank you.

Cutting Mat – Any size mat will be fine as you are mainly trimming smaller blocks, but just make sure it has inches marked on it. My advice would be to get one to fit your flat space and budget. I find it easier to cut out fabric at a kitchen workspace height, rather than sitting down.

Square patchwork ruler – I use a 6 ½" x 6 ½" ruler, which is great for most blocks I make. I do have a larger one but it is a bit cumbersome. You are looking for a square ruler that has a 45-degree line through the middle and where one of the corners has two 1" markers.

¼" Patchwork foot – Patchwork is all about the ¼" seam and being consistent with your seams. For this reason you will need a ¼" patchwork foot. There are two types of these: one with a guide and one without. The one without the guide is better for making Half Square Triangles as you will be sewing ¼" away from a drawn line. The ones with the fabric guides are slightly better for piecing your blocks together because they allow you to line the side up with the edge of the fabric. You can buy generic ones, which are compatible with most sewing machines, relatively cheaply online. You don't need both, I personally use the one without the guide.

Iron & Ironing board – Nothing beyond a standard iron and ironing board is required. I hardly ever used the iron before I started patchwork, but now it's become part of my daily routine!

Seam Ripper – Mistakes are unavoidable and I still make plenty of them. Always keep a seam ripper within reach.

Basting Pins / Spray – When it comes to joining the three layers of quilt together, you'll need to secure them with something. I'm a big fan of the basting spray, which is an aerosol glue spray that disappears with water.

It doesn't stick them together completely, so you can still move the layers a little if you spot a crease. The alternative is to use basting pins, which are curved safety pins. I know lots of people who use this method and prefer it. It's really all about what works for you.

EXTRA FUN TOOLS I USE

Snazzy Rulers – There are lots of other speciality rulers on the market and what you use tends to come down to personal preference and budget. I love my Bloc-Loc rulers for trimming Half Square Triangles (HSTs) and Flying Geese. They are not cheap, but if you are going to patchwork regularly I think they are worth it.

Rotating Cutting mat – I only got one of these a few months ago and I think it is fab. They are little square or circular cutting mats that rotate, so when you are trimming all sides of your HSTs they save quite a bit of time. Instead of having to pick up the block and turn it, you just nudge the mat around.

Flatter Spray – It's a natural starch that you spray on your fabric when ironing. It helps to get creases out and can really help flatten seams. It isn't a stiff starch at all, your fabric still feels the same, just flatter and less creased. It also smells amazing, which may be the real reason I use lots of it!

TECHNIQUES

The ¼" Seam - Probably the most important aspect of patchwork is using a ¼" seam, if all of your blocks are pieced together using a ¼" seam then you know they will all be exactly the same size. It's important that your blocks are the correct size so that they fit nicely together and using the consistent seam helps this. Most patchwork patterns use a ¼" seam and pattern maths take this in to account. It took me a while to get used to working in inches, (I am a metric girl!) but after a while it starts to make sense.

Finished and Unfinished size blocks - You will find lots of references to unfinished and finished sizes, especially in cutting out instructions. Simply explained:
The finished size is the size of the block once it has been sewn in.
The unfinished size is the size before you sew it in.
The unfinished size will be ½" bigger than the unfinished size as you will be sewing a ¼" seam on each side.

Ironing Seams - There are two main types of seam ironing that you will do, and the pattern will usually tell you which one is required. You may develop a preference and sometimes a pattern might not specify, so just do what feels right to you.
Iron seam open – Slightly obvious this one, just open up the seam and iron it flat. Mainly used when seams are getting a bit bulky.
Closed seams – You keep the seam together and either iron it flat towards the left or right-hand side. This is used for nestling seams together when sewing rows. It is also used when making Half Square Triangles. If one side is light fabric then you iron the seam towards the darker fabric, so you don't see it through the top.

OTHER ABBREVIATIONS YOU ARE LIKELY TO COME ACROSS
WOF Width of fabric. This generally means the full width of a 42/44" quilting cotton.

RST Right sides together. This is used when you are placing two pieces of fabric together in order to sew a seam. The right side refers to the printed side of the fabric.

WST Wrong sides together. This means that the fabric is placed so that the underside (non-printed) sides of the fabric are touching.

HST Half Square Triangle. The HST is a block that I use a lot in quilt design and you can find out more about it in the tutorial pages.

Wadding This is the layer of warm padding that goes in the middle of the quilt layers, it can sometimes be referred to as batting.

FQ Fat Quarter of fabric. Lots of fabric comes in fat quarters and you can get some great fat quarter bundles. If you are buying in metres then a fat quarter is 50cm in length by half the width of the fabric, so approximately 56cm. If you are buying in yards then it is 18" in length by half the width of the fabric, so approximately 21".

F8 Fat Eight of fabric. A fat eight of fabric is half of a fat quarter so approximately 56cm x 25cm or in inches it's 9" x 21".

chapter two: tutorials

*With the basics under your belt, it's time to step things up a level. This section will
teach you the key skills required to help bring your patchwork ideas to life, before
you get started on your first project...*

TIP Before I baste this layer,
I place the quilt top on the
wadding to make sure that the
bottom two pieces are
big enough

So now we've grasped some of the basics let's look in more detail at some
of the skills you will need. These tutorials cover the instructions for making
specific blocks like Half Square Triangles, Flying Geese and Diamonds in
Squares. As well as blocks we'll cover the all-important finishing touches
like basting, quilting and binding quilts and making an envelope cushion.
The individual projects will guide you back to these tutorials, so use them
as a useful reference guide.

BASTING QUILTS

The finished quilt is made from three layers: the quilt top, the wadding (or
batting) and the quilt backing. Before you can quilt your project, you need
to baste the three layers together. I very much prefer spray basting using
something like 505 Spray.

It is really important to get all layers smooth so that you get a good finish.
I baste quilts on the floor, thankfully I don't have carpets, so I can use
masking tape. If crawling around on the floor is a bit much for you, a wall
would also work. This is how I baste:

STEP 1 Iron the quilt top and quilt backing so that they are nice and crease
free. You also need to remove as many loose threads as you can.

STEP 2 Take your quilt backing and lay it out on the floor with the wrong
side facing up. Take some making tape (I use a thick painter's tape) and
mask the top and bottom edge to the floor, making sure it is held in place
flatly and tightly.

STEP 3 If there is some movement in the fabric widthways you can also
add some masking tape to the sides too. The tighter and less creased
you get this bottom layer the better the finish will be so it is worth taking
your time.

STEP 4 Once you are happy with the bottom layer, place the wadding on
top. Make sure that it covers the quilt backing.

STEP 5 To baste the wadding to the quilt backing, roll back about 10"
of wadding from the top and lightly spray your basting spray on to the
quilt back. Carefully fold the wadding back on top of the sprayed area,
smoothing out any creases as you go.

STEP 6 Once the top 10″ is basted then you fold the remaining wadding back over this and spray another 10″ section just below. Again, carefully fold back the wadding and smooth it out.

STEP 7 Continue basting the wadding to the quilt backing in 10″ increments, smoothing it out each time.

STEP 8 Once the bottom two layers are basted lay the quilt top right side up on top of the wadding. Make sure that there are a couple of inches extra backing and wadding each side of the quilt top. Baste the quilt top in the same way you basted the wadding to the backing.

QUILTING YOUR QUILT

There are lots of options for quilting, use one that you feel comfortable with. The main options are Straight Line (Walking Foot) quilting and Free Motion quilting. My preference is for Straight Line quilting.

Straight Line Quilting This technique uses your walking foot, which feeds the top and bottom fabric evenly through the machine. Some machines come with a walking foot or with Dual Feed built in, but, if you don't have a walking foot it is worth investing in one if you want to use your machine for straight line quilting. There are lots of options when using the Walking Foot, my favourite is to quilt straight lines across the quilt, either diagonally, horizontally or vertically, using the side of the foot to keep my lines equally spaced. You can also use the walking foot to echo quilt, this means sewing a set distance away from the blocks to highlight certain shapes like stars. The more you use this method

the more ideas you will come up with and there are some fantastic learning resources online and in books.

Free Motion Quilting This method uses a Free Motion foot on your machine in combination with lowering the Feed Dogs. You then control the fabric as it moves through the sewing machine. This means that the fabric can go in any direction and you are in control. You can create lots of patterns, including, swirls, circles and loops. There are unlimited possibilities and some fantastic books specialising in the technique. It definitely takes some practice and is not something I have yet mastered but I will keep practising.

Long Arm Quilting There are special sewing machines that use a frame for the quilt and have a long arm for the quilting. The machines are large and expensive but plenty of businesses offer long arm quilting as a service. I have a wonderful long arm quilter (Worktown Quilts) I use to You can specify the design or let the long arm quilter come up with a custom design for you. Along with the benefit of not quilting it yourself you also don't need to baste your quilt as it is attached to the frame and stretched tight.

BINDING YOUR QUILT

I use a 2½" width of fabric strips to make my binding, which gives plenty of fold over. It is easy to make your binding as it doesn't require you to cut on the bias, unless you are making something circular. When I first started quilting, binding was the stage I found the trickiest as I kept forgetting how to do it. The more you do it though, the easier it becomes, so if you haven't done it before just keep going and it will be second nature before you know it. Before you start attaching your binding remember to trim the excess wadding and backing fabric from your quilt and square it up.

To make binding:

STEP 1 Cut the required number of 2½" strips of fabric. I use full Width of Fabric (WOF) strips so that I have fewer joins.

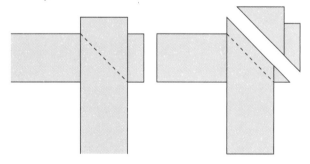

Fig 1.   **Fig 2.**

STEP 2 You now need to join the strips together to make one long piece of binding. To do this place one strip end at a 90-degree angle with the end of another strip, RST. Draw a 45-degree line from the top left corner to the bottom right where the strips meet. (Fig 1)

STEP 3 Sew along the drawn line and then trim away the excess ¼" past the seam. When you have done this, iron the seam open. (Fig 2)

STEP 4 Repeat until all of the strips are joined together. Fold the binding in half lengthways, WST and iron.

Attaching your binding

My biggest tip for attaching you binding is to go slowly, I use the speed dial on my machine to force me to be a bit slower.

Fig 3.

STEP 5 Starting about a third down from a corner and leaving approx. 6" to 8" of binding loose match up the raw edge of your folded binding with the edge of the quilt sandwich. Use a ¼" seam to sew the binding to the quilt, making sure you sew backwards at the start of the seam to lock your stitches. (Fig 3)

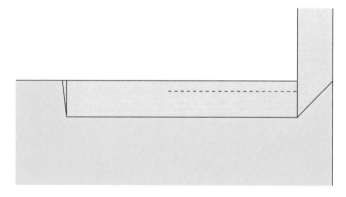

Fig 4.

STEP 6 When you get to a corner stop ¼" from the edge and backstitch to lock your stitches before cutting your threads. Rotate your quilt sandwich so the next edge is on the right-hand side. Fold the binding upwards past the quilt sandwich. (Fig 4)

Fig 5.

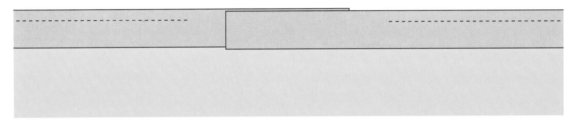

Fig 6.

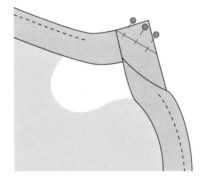

Fig 7.

STEP 7 Fold back the binding strip towards you, which will give you a folded triangle in the middle. Start sewing ¼" from the top edge, backstitching again to lock stitches. Carry on until the next corner and repeat. (Fig 5)

STEP 8 Once you get back to the beginning stop approx. 12" from the start and backstitch.

Joining your binding strips

The simple way to join the binding strips is to fold over the starting edge and tuck the end piece in before sewing down the ends. This is nice and simple but can be a bit bulky. A better way is to join the ends of the binding strips, in the same way you made the binding strips.

STEP 9 Cut the end of the last binding strip so that it overlaps the starting piece by 2 ½", or the starting width of your binding if you used a different size of binding strips. (Fig 6)

STEP 10 Open the binding strip and match up them up RST at a right angle. Draw or mark a diagonal line from one corner to the other and then pin in place. (Fig 7)

STEP 11 Sew along the marked line to join the binding strips and then cut away the excess triangle by trimming ¼" away from the sewn line.

STEP 12 Press the seam open and then re-fold the binding. Match up the raw edges of the binding with the outer edge of the quilt and then sew down with a ¼" seam to finish.

Finishing your binding

To finish attaching the binding to the quilt fold the binding over the edge and on to the back of the quilt. Using a small slip stitch, hand stitch the binding to the backing fabric. Using thread that matches the binding will help hide your stitches.

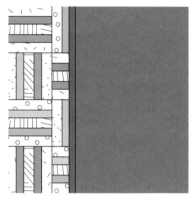

Fig 1.

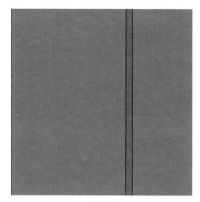

Fig 2.

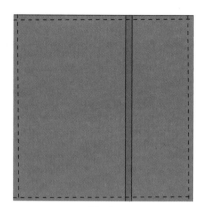

Fig 3.

MAKING AN ENVELOPE CUSHION

I like to make envelope cushions as they are nice and easy and there are no tricky hidden zips or button holes. I tend to make my cushion covers ½" smaller than the actual cushion inner, which helps to make the cushion nice and bouncy.

Preparing your cushion top

All of the projects in this book suggest quilting the cushion top. It is optional whether you create a quilt sandwich with your top by adding a backing fabric. In theory the back of your wadding won't be seen inside the cushion, so you can leave it unbacked, but I like to hide it by adding backing fabric. If you want to add backing fabric do this before you start quilting.

I just use some pins to baste the top unless it is a large cushion top, in which case, I will spray baste. Once you have the top basted, then you need to quilt it. The patterns give you an idea on how I did it, normally in simple straight lines or by echoing the design. I really like quilting cushions as they are smaller than quilts, and really easy to move about under the machine.

Preparing the back of the cushion

Some of the patterns in the book have quilted backs, where the two pieces are basted and quilted separately before finishing off one edge on each with binding. Some of the quilts use pieces of heavy weight canvas or denim as cushion back fabric, which doesn't require quilting, just either binding or hemming. You can use the method for each project or swap around.

Making the cushion

STEP 1 Once you have your two backing pieces made, place the first piece RST with the cushion top so that the raw edges are aligned, and the hemmed piece is on top of the cushion piece. (Fig.1)

STEP 2 Take the second backing piece and line it up on the opposite side, the two hemmed edges will overlap by about a third of the cushion width. This is what gives the envelope. (Fig 2)

STEP 3 Pin or clip these three pieces together around all of the edges, if the top and back are slightly different in size (it happens) then trim away any excess from the cushion backs. Sew around all of the edges of the cushion with a ¼" seam, making sure you backstitch at the start and end. Trim the corners carefully. (Fig 3)

STEP 4 All you need to do now is reach inside and pull the cushion right-side out through the envelope opening.

TIP If you want to hide the raw edges inside the cushion you can sew binding over the edges, just make sure not to sew past the seam line.

HALF SQUARE TRIANGLE TUTORIAL

I love Half Square Triangles (HSTs) they are so versatile and are the foundation for most of the patterns I design. They are really simple to make and with method 3 you can make eight HSTs in one go. I like to make my HSTs a little bit bigger than needed so that I can trim them to size. The instructions for HSTs in my book include this extra size, so they will need trimming to the unfinished size.

Method 1. Half Square Triangles (two at a time)

This is my go-to method for making HSTs, unless I'm making lots of the same HSTs then it's all about method 3. This was the first method I tried and it is really simple to do.

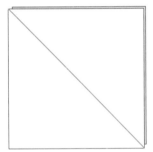

Fig 1.

STEP 1 On one of the squares and using a ruler, draw a line diagonally from one corner to the opposite corner. Note: This will be on the wrong side of the fabric. (Fig 1)

STEP 2 Place the marked fabric RST with the second square that makes up the HSTs.

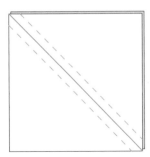

Fig 2.

STEP 3 Sew ¼" away from both sides of the marked line. You will be sewing two lines in total. (Fig 2)

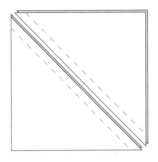

Fig 3.

STEP 4 Once you have sewn the two lines cut along the central line you drew, you now have two HSTs. (Fig 3)

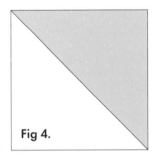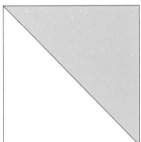

Fig 4.

STEP 5 Once trimmed, open up the HSTs and iron the seams towards the darker fabric. (Fig 4)

HSTs two at a time cutting and trimming guide		
HST Finished Size	Starting Squares	Trim to (unfinished size)
2"	3¼"	2½"
3"	4¼"	3½"
4"	5¼"	4½"
5"	6¼"	5½"
6"	7¼"	6½"
7"	8¼"	7½"
8"	9¼"	8½"

Method 2
Half Square Triangles (four at a time)

This method is fast and requires no fabric marking. The only downside is that the edges of your HSTs will be on the bias, so be careful when sewing them in as they will be prone to stretching.

Fig 1.   **Fig 2.**

STEP 1 Place the two squares, which make up the HSTs, together (RST). Sew around the edges of the square with a ¼" seam. (Fig 1)

STEP 2 Cut the square diagonally into four triangles. (Fig 2)

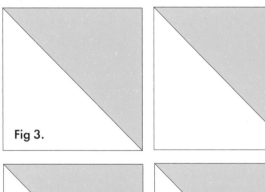

Fig 3.

STEP 3 Once trimmed, open up the four HSTs and iron the seam towards the darker fabric. (Fig 3)

HSTs four at a time cutting and trimming guide		
HST Finished Size	Starting Squares	Trim to (unfinished size)
2"	4 ¼"	2½"
3"	5 ¾"	3 ½"
4"	7 ¼"	4 ½"
5"	8 ¾"	5 ½"
6"	10"	6 ½"
7"	11 ½"	7 ½"
8"	13"	8 ½"

Method 3
Half Square Triangles (eight at a time)

Great when you have lots of the same HSTs to make, it will use less fabric and save time. I suggest this method for a few quilts in this book and it's really easy to do.

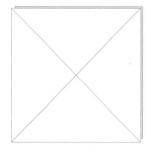
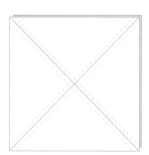

Fig 1.   **Fig 2.**

STEP 1 On the wrong side of one of the squares, use a ruler to draw two lines diagonally across the fabric, one going left-to-right and one right-to-left. (Fig 1)

STEP 2 Place the marked fabric RST with the second square that makes up the HSTs.

STEP 3 Sew ¼" away from both sides of the marked lines, sewing four lines in total. (Fig 2)

STEP 4 Cut the fabrics horizontally and vertically through the middle to give four pairs of HSTs. (Fig 3)

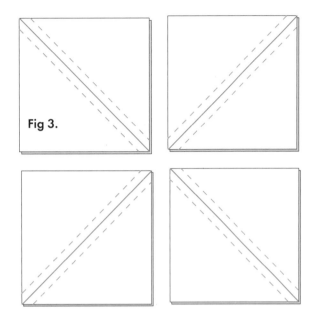

Fig 3.

HSTs eight at a time cutting and trimming guide

HST Finished Size	Starting Squares	Trim to (unfinished size)
2″	6″	2½″
3″	8″	3 ½″
4″	10″	4 ½″
5″	12″	5 ½″
6″	14″	6 ½″
7″	16″	7 ½″
8″	18″	8 ½″

Trimming Half Square Triangles

I like to make my HSTs larger than needed and trim them to size accurately. You can make HSTs to the correct size, but no matter how hard I try I can never make them perfect without trimming.

STEP 1 Take your patchwork ruler and place it so that the corner with the 1″ marker on each side is at the top.

STEP 2 Find the measurement you need down the left-hand side, for this example it is 4½″. Line this up with the left-hand side of the un-opened HST seam.

STEP 5 Cut open each HST pair by cutting along the drawn line, then once trimmed, iron open the eight HSTs to finish. (Fig 4)

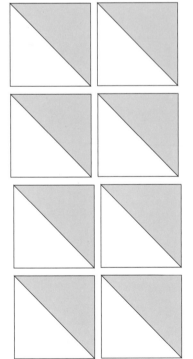

Fig 4.

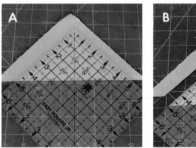
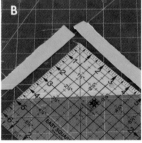

STEP 3 Move the ruler so the same measurement on the right-hand side is lined up with the right-hand side of the seam. (photo A)

STEP 4 Trim along the two sides and iron open the HST. (photo B)

TIP If trimming lots of the same sized HSTs, mark this diagonal line with washi tape. It saves working out where the measurements are each time.

FLYING GEESE TUTORIAL

Flying Geese are rectangular blocks with a large triangle (the Goose) and two little triangles (the sky). They can be made by sewing triangles together, but I prefer to use rectangles and squares as my starting points. There are two methods, the one at a time method and the no waste four at a time method. Unlike HSTs the Flying Geese don't need trimming, although you can get speciality rulers to make them and trim them, if you prefer utter perfection.

Method 1
Flying Geese (one at a time)

This method is a simple way to make Flying Geese. If you are making lots, then I would suggest the no waste method. This method uses 2 small squares and one rectangle.

STEP 1 On the wrong side of the two small squares and using a ruler, draw a line diagonally across the fabric on each square.

Fig 1.

STEP 2 Take the rectangle and line up one of the small squares with the left-hand edge of the rectangle. Remember to place the fabrics RST Sew along the line you have drawn. (Fig 1)

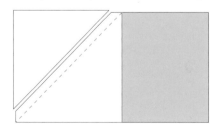

Fig 2.

STEP 3 Cut away the excess ¼" away from the sewn line. (Fig 2)

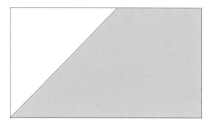

Fig 3.

STEP 4 Fold out the small triangle and iron the seams outwards. (Fig 3)

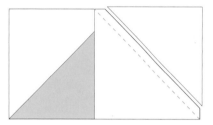

Fig 4.

STEP 5 Repeat steps 1 to 4 with the second square but placing it on the right-hand side of the rectangle. (Fig 4)

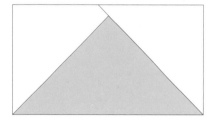

Fig 5.

STEP 6 Fold second small triangle and iron the seams outwards, giving you a Flying Geese unit. (Fig 5)

Flying Geese one at a time cutting guide			
FG Finished size	FG Unfinished size	(x1) Large rectangle	(x2) Squares
1" x 2"	1½" x 2½"	1½" x 2½"	1½"
2" x 4"	2½" x 4½"	2½" x 4½"	2½"
3" x 6"	3½" x 6½"	3½" x 6½"	3½"
4" x 8"	4½" x 8½"	4½" x 8½"	4½"
5" x 10"	5½" x 10½"	5½" x 10½"	5½"

Method 2
Flying Geese (four at a time no waste method)

This method is great when you have lots of the same Flying Geese to make and is used in some of the patterns. If definitely saves on the number of little squares you need to cut up and there are no little triangles left over.

STEP 1 On the wrong side of the small squares and using a ruler, draw a line diagonally across the fabric on each square.

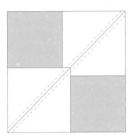 

Fig 1.   **Fig 2.**

STEP 2 Take the large square and place the smaller squares in two of the corners, diagonally opposite. Sew a line ¼" away from the drawn line on each side. (Fig 1)

STEP 3 Cut along the drawn line so that you now have two blocks. (Fig 2)

 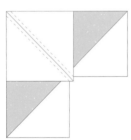

Fig 3.   **Fig 4.**

STEP 4 On each of the blocks press the seams towards the small triangles. (Fig 3)

STEP 5 Place one of the small squares in the remaining corner of the large square, so the drawn line goes from the corner to where the small triangles meet. Sew a line ¼" away from the drawn line on each side. (Fig 4)

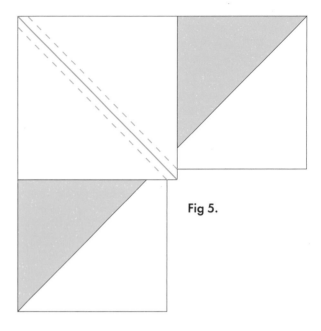

Fig 5.

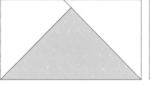 

Fig 6.

STEP 6 Cut along the drawn line (Fig 5) and then iron open the triangles so you have two Flying Geese units. (Fig 6)

STEP 7 Repeat with the other block, from STEP 3.

Flying Geese four at a time cutting guide			
FG Finished size	FG Unfinished size	(x1) Large square	(x4) Small squares
1" x 2"	1½" x 2½"	3¼"	1⅞"
2" x 4"	2½" x 4½	5¼"	2⅞"
3" x 6"	3½" x 6½"	7¼"	3⅞"
4" x 8"	4½" x 8½"	9¼"	4⅞"
5" x 10"	5½" x 10½"	11¼"	5⅞"

DIAMOND IN SQUARE

These blocks are fairly simple to make and can add a really strong look to a quilt design. They are made from one large central square plus two smaller outer squares, which are cut in two diagonally to create four triangles.

STEP 1 Take two small squares and cut each one in half diagonally.

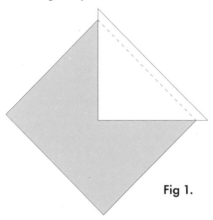

Fig 1.

STEP 2 Take the large square and place one of the triangles so that the long edge matches up with one of the square edges, the point of the triangle will be pointing in towards the square. Make sure the triangle is centred with the square, there will be ¼" hanging over each side. Sew a seam ¼" in from the matched-up edge. (Fig 1)

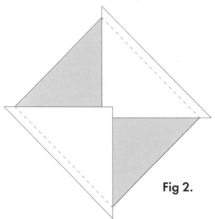

Fig 2.

STEP 3 Repeat for the opposite edge of the square.

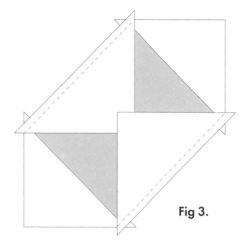

Fig 3.

STEP 4 Press open the two completed sides outwards and then line up the remaining two triangles with the other square edges. (Fig 3)

Fig 4.

STEP 5 Press the seams outwards and you have a finished block. (Fig 4)

Diamond in a square cutting guide			
Finished size	Unfinished size	(1x) Centre square	Small squares
3"	3½"	2⅝"	2⅜"
4"	4½"	3⅜"	2⅞"
5"	5½"	4"	3⅜"
6"	6½"	4¾"	3⅞"
7"	7½"	5½"	4⅜"
8"	8½"	6⅛"	4⅞"

chapter three: quilt projects

There are six quilt projects included for you to make, ranging from simple lap quilts to larger bed quilts. The projects use a variety of blocks from the tutorial pages, giving you lots of opportunities to practise new skills! There are seriously bright rainbows, more muted rainbows and, for fans of the 80s, a fabulous neon rainbow. I've also included some colouring pages, so you can play around with your own combinations...

vintage stars double quilt

I had really good fun choosing the fabric for this quilt. I don't always use strong prints but I wanted a vintage look that used fabrics I stashed whilst on holiday. My husband wasn't so pleased as he had to carry them 10 miles across Boston!

Size: 84" x 84"

Quilt Top Fabric:

- ▦ 1 ¼ Yards (1 ¼m) each of Bright Red and Orange

- ▦ 1 Yard each (1m) each of Bright Yellow, Green, Blue, Purple and Pink

- ▦ ¾ Yard (¾m) each of Low volume Red, Orange, Yellow, Green, Blue, Purple and Pink

Finishing Fabric:

- ▦ ¾ Yard (¾m) Binding Fabric

- ▦ 5 Yards (4¾m) Backing Fabric

- ▦ 90"(2.3m) square, Wadding

CUTTING INSTRUCTIONS

From the Bright Red fabric, cut;
(x5) 6½" WOF strips – sub cut into (x27) 6½" squares
(x2) 3⅞" WOF strips – sub cut into (x14) 3⅞" squares

From the Bright Orange fabric, cut;
(x5) 6½" WOF strips – sub cut into (x27) 6½" squares
(x2) 3⅞" WOF strips – sub cut into (x14) 3⅞" squares

From the Bright Yellow fabric, cut;
(x4) 6½" WOF strips – sub cut into (x23) 6½" squares
(x2) 3⅞" WOF strips – sub cut into (x12) 3⅞" squares

From the Bright Green fabric, cut;
(x4) 6½" WOF strips – sub cut into (x19) 6½" squares
(x1) 3⅞" WOF strips – sub cut into (x10) 3⅞" squares

From the Bright Blue fabric, cut;
(x3) 6½" WOF strips – sub cut into (x18) 6½" squares
(x1) 3⅞" WOF strips – sub cut into (x8) 3⅞" squares

From the Bright Purple fabric, cut;
(x4) 6½" WOF strips – sub cut into (x19) 6½" squares
(x1) 3⅞" WOF strips – sub cut into (x10) 3⅞" squares

From the Bright Pink fabric, cut;
(x4) 6½" WOF strips – sub cut into (x23) 6½" squares
(x2) 3⅞" WOF strips – sub cut into (x12) 3⅞" squares

From the Red Low volume fabric, cut;
(x5) 3½" WOF strips – sub cut into (x54) 3½" squares
(x1) 4¾" WOF strips – sub cut into (x7) 4¾" squares

From the Orange Low volume fabric, cut;
(x5) 3½" WOF strips – sub cut into (x54) 3½" squares
(x1) 4¾" WOF strips – sub cut into (x7) 4¾" squares

From the Yellow Low volume fabric, cut;
(x4) 3½" WOF strips – sub cut into (x46) 3½" squares
(x1) 4¾" WOF strips – sub cut into (x6) 4¾" squares

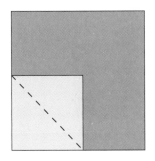

Fig 1.

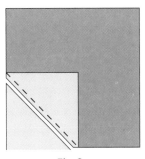

Fig 2.

Fig 3.

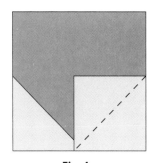

Fig 4.

From the Green Low volume fabric, cut;
(x4) 3½" WOF strips – sub cut into (x38) 3½" squares
(x1) 4¾" WOF strips – sub cut into (x5) 4¾" squares
From the Blue Low volume fabric, cut;
(x3) 3½" WOF strips – sub cut into (x36) 3½" squares
(x1) 4¾" WOF strips – sub cut into (x4) 4¾" squares
From the Purple Low volume fabric, cut;
(x4) 3½" WOF strips – sub cut into (x38) 3½" squares
(x1) 4¾" WOF strips – sub cut into (x5) 4¾" squares
From the Pink Low volume fabric, cut;
(x4) 3½" WOF strips – sub cut into (x46) 3½" squares
(x1) 4¾" WOF strips – sub cut into (x6) 4¾" squares

QUILT BLOCKS

There are two types of blocks used in this quilt.
Block A is a diamond in square block and Block B is
the pointed square, which forms the cross shape in
the quilt.

BLOCK A: DIAMOND IN SQUARE

Each diamond in square unit is made with one 4¾"
Low volume centre square and two darker 3⅞"
squares (cut diagonally across) for the outer triangles.
STEP 1 Following the instructions on the tutorial page
27, to make the diamond in square blocks below.
Each will measure 6½" square (unfinished size).
(x7) Red / Low volume Red
(x7) Orange / Low volume Orange
(x6) Yellow / Low volume Yellow

(x5) Green / Low volume Green
(x4) Blue / Low volume Blue
(x5) Purple / Low volume Purple
(x6) Pink / Low volume Pink

BLOCK B: POINTED SQUARE

The pointed squares are created in a similar way to
Flying Geese and form the crosses when the rows are
sewn together. They are simple to make and don't
require any trimming. I've also included a handy hint
later if you want to create lots of little HSTs at the
same time.
STEP 2 Take a 6½" Blue square and place a 3½" Blue
Low volume square in the bottom left corner, so that
the outer edges are lined up. Draw a line diagonally
across the 3½" square as shown in Fig 1 and sew
along the drawn line. (Fig 1)
STEP 3 Trim away the excess fabric a ¼" from the
sewn line (Fig 2) - (or follow the handy hint below
in STEP 7).
STEP 4 Open out the triangle and press the seam
open. (Fig 3)
STEP 5 Place the second Blue Low volume square on
to the bottom right hand corner and draw a diagonal
line across it. (Fig 4)
STEP 6 Sew along the drawn line and then trim ¼"
away from the sewn line and press open. (Fig 5)
STEP 7 Matching the 6½" coloured squares and the
3½" Low volume squares, you need to create the

Fig 5.

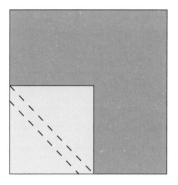

Fig 6.

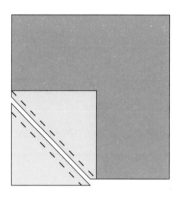

Fig 7.

following Cross blocks:
(x27) Red / Low volume Red blocks
(x27) Orange / Low volume Orange blocks
(x23) Yellow / Low volume Yellow blocks
(x19) Green / Low volume Green blocks
(x18) Blue / Low volume Blue blocks
(x19) Purple / Low volume Purple blocks
(x23) Pink / Low volume Pink blocks

Handy hint - If like me you hate to waste fabric and the thought of lots spare triangles is too much to bear, then you can make them into HSTs ready for another project. I used the spare HSTs made to make the cushion, and I still have lots left for another scrappy project.

After you have sewn on the drawn lines, simply;
1. Sew another line ½" outside of that line. (Fig 6)
2. Trim the triangle between the two sewn lines, which will be ¼" from each one. (Fig 7)
3. Open up both parts and you will have the block you were making plus a HST.

PUTTING THE TOP TOGETHER

STEP 8 Once you have all of the blocks made up, you may want to layout the blocks on the floor. I always find it helpful to take a photo that I can refer to as a double check when sewing the rows together. Use the layout diagram as a guide.

STEP 9 If you have laid out your quilt, then collect the rows and label them (this really does make it easier). Starting with row 1, sew each block together with a ¼" seam, double checking that the block is orientated in the correct direction.

STEP 10 Sew each row in turn and press all of the seams open. I find it really helpful to label my rows at this point.

STEP 11 Making sure you are matching the seams, sew together the rows to form the quilt top.

FINISHING YOUR QUILT

STEP 12 If using normal width quilting cotton (approx. 44") you will need to cut a 5 yard piece of fabric in half, creating two 2½ yard long pieces. Cut away the selvedge and then join the two pieces together with a ½" seam. Iron open the seam.

STEP 13 Give the backing fabric and quilt top a good press and baste using your preferred method.

STEP 14 Quilt as desired, I chose to get this one professionally long arm quilted, with a star and swirl pattern all over. You could do some simple straight lines across the width of the quilt instead.

STEP 15 Join your binding strips together using a 45-degree angle and then attach to the quilt. See the binding tutorial for help if needed.

ALTERNATIVES

You could make a really scrappy version of this quilt and have every cross block in different fabrics. Each full cross block uses just under a fat eighth of Bright fabric and approximately a fat eighth of Low volume fabric. It is definitely on my list to make another version of this quilt using all of those lonely fat quarters I have. Use the colouring in page to help you with your layout, and I would absolutely make sure you label your rows.

QUILT LAYOUT DIAGRAM

COLOURING PAGE

racing stripes lap quilt

I wanted to create a nice and simple rainbow gradient quilt, and nothing is quite so simple as stripes. The quilt used all 14 colours of the colour wheel, with two shades of the main rainbow colours. Choosing plain fabrics meant that I could get all of the colours and shades. The name racing stripes is a little nod to the time my Mum got 'go faster' stripes put on her car. It didn't go faster!

Size: 42" x 58"

Quilt Top Fabric:
- Long FQ each of the Main, Red, Orange, Yellow, Green, Blue, Purple and Pink
- F8 each of Light Red, Light-Orange, Light-Yellow, Light-Green, Light-Blue, Light-Purple and Light-Pink
- Long FQ each of Mid-colours, Red-Orange, Orange-Yellow, Yellow-Green, Green-Blue, Blue-Purple, Purple-Pink and Pink-Red
- 1¼ Yards (1¼m) Low Volume Background Fabric

Finishing Fabric:
- ½ Yard (½m) Binding fabric
- 2⅔ Yards (2½m) Backing fabric
- 50" x 64" (1.3m x 1.65m) wadding

CUTTING INSTRUCTIONS

From each of the seven main fabrics, e.g. Red, cut;
(x2) 2½ in x 36½ in strips

From each of the seven Light colour fabrics, e.g. Light-Red, cut;
(x2) 2½ in x 8½ in rectangles

From each of the seven Mid-colour fabrics, e.g. Red-Orange, cut;
(x1) 1½ in x 36½ in strip

From the background fabric cut;
(x14) 1 in x 36½ in strips
(x8) 2½ in x 42½ in strips
(x7) 2½ in x 6½ in rectangles

From the Binding fabric, cut;
(x6) 2½ in WOF Strips

QUILT BLOCKS

There are three main blocks in the quilt plus background strips. There are two types of Light/Dark colour blocks, Block A and Block B, they differ depending on the direction of the join. In addition, there is Block C, the mid-colour striped block that sits between a Block A and Block B.

Block A where the diagonal join between darker main fabric and light fabric runs from the bottom to the top, in a right-hand direction.
Block B where the diagonal join between darker main fabric and light fabric runs from the bottom to the top in a left-hand direction.
Block C goes between a Block A and Block B to create the racing stripe.

CREATING BLOCK A

STEP 1 Place the Light-Blue (2½" x 8½") rectangle right side up horizontally. Place the main Blue (2½" x 36½") strip RST at a 90-degree angle, running vertically up. Draw a line from the bottom left corner of the

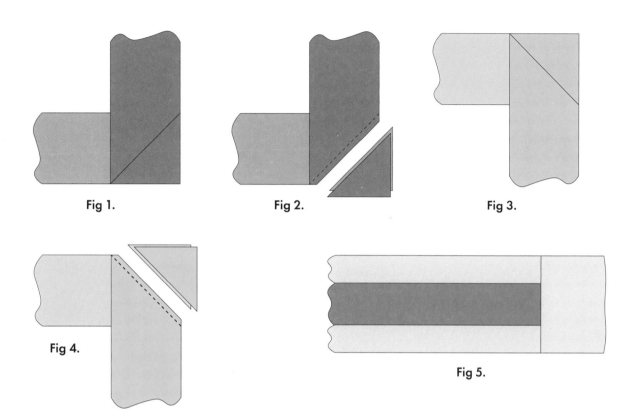

Fig 1.   Fig 2.   Fig 3.

Fig 4.   Fig 5.

top fabric to the top corner where they meet. (Fig 1) Pin in place and then sew along the marked line.

STEP 2 Once you have sewn the line trim ¼" away from the line to trim off the edge and iron open the seam. (Fig 2)

STEP 3 Repeat the steps above so that you have the following blocks:

(x2) Red / Light-Red strips

(x1) Orange / Light-Orange strips

(x1) Green / Light-Green strips

(x2) Blue / Light-Blue strips

(x1) Purple / Light-Purple strips

CREATING BLOCK B

STEP 4 Place the Light-Yellow (2½" x 8½") rectangle right side up horizontally. Place the main Yellow (2½" x 36½") strip RST at a 90-degree angle running vertically downwards. Draw a line from the top left corner of the top fabric to the bottom right corner

where they meet. (Fig 3)

STEP 5 Pin in place and then sew along the marked line. Once you have sewn the line trim ¼" away from the line to trim off the edge. (Fig 4)

STEP 6 Repeat steps above, so you have these blocks:

(x1) Orange / Light-Orange strip

(x2) Yellow / Light-Yellow strips

(x1) Green / Light-Green strip

(x1) Purple / Light-Purple strip

(x2) Pink / Light-Purple strips

CREATING BLOCK C

STEP 7 Sew the Green-Blue (1½" x 36½") strip between the two (1" x 36½") background fabric strips using a ¼" seam.

STEP 8 Press open the seams and then add a (2½" x 6½") background fabric rectangle to the right-hand side of the striped block. (Fig 5)

STEP 9 Repeat STEPS 7 & 8 so that you have one

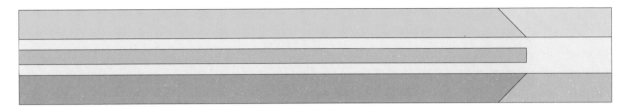

Fig 6. Right facing stripe

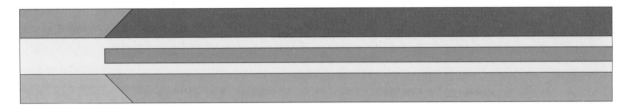

Fig 7. Left facing stripe

block C for each of the seven mid colours.

PUTTING THE TOP TOGETHER

Each racing stripe is comprised of a Block A, B and C; with Block C in the centre. The background end of Block C joins up with the Light ends of Blocks A and B.

Right Facing Stripes – Block B on top

Block B: Yellow, Block C: Yellow-Green, Block A: Green

Block B: Pink, Block C: Pink-Red, Block A: Red

Block B: Green, Block C: Green-Blue, Block A: Blue

Left Facing Stripes – Block A on top

Block A: Red, Block C: Red-Orange, Block B: Orange

Block A: Blue, Block C: Blue-Purple, Block B: Purple

Block A: Orange, Block C: Orange-Yellow, Block B: Yellow

Block A: Purple, Block C: Purple-Pink, Block B: Pink

STEP 10 To make the right facing racing stripe in Fig 6 sew together a Green Block A, Yellow Block A and a Yellow-Green Block C. Make sure that the Yellow Block B is at the top and the Green Block A is at the bottom and that the arrow design is pointing towards the right.

STEP 11 Press the seams open when finished.

STEP 12 To make the left facing racing stripe in Fig 7 sew together a Red Block A, Orange Block B and a Red-Orange Block C. Make sure that the Red Block A is at the top and the Orange Block B is at the bottom and that the arrow design is pointing towards the left.

STEP 13 Press the seams open when finished.

STEP 14 Repeat the steps above to create all of the combinations of racing stripes needed, using the quilt layout diagram to check the direction of the arrows, if needed.

STEP 15 This is a very simple quilt to sew together once the racing stripes are made. Simply sew the rows together, alternating racing stripes and the plain background 2½" WOF strips, as per the layout diagram.

STEP 16 Trim up the quilt top sides, ensuring all of the rows are the same width.

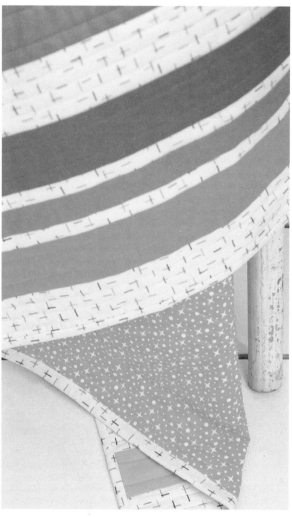

FINISHING YOUR QUILT

STEP 17 If using normal width quilting cotton (approx. 44") you will need to cut a 2⅔ Yard piece of fabric in half, creating (x2) 1⅓ Yard long pieces. Cut away the selvedge and then join the two pieces together with a ½" seam. Iron open the seam.

STEP 18 Give the backing fabric and quilt top a good press and baste using your preferred method.

STEP 19 Quilt your quilt; I used straight line quilting to quilt across the stripes, changing my thread to match the stripe colours. It was a really simple and effective way to add extra depth to the stripes.

STEP 20 Join your binding strips together using a 45-degree angle and then attach to the quilt. See the binding tutorial for help if needed.

ALTERNATIVES

You can of course change the colour scheme to suit. It is also a great quilt to make with Jelly roll strips as a way to show off your favourite collection of fabrics. This quilt is easy to re-size, just make the stripes longer or keep adding stripes to the bottom of the quilt.

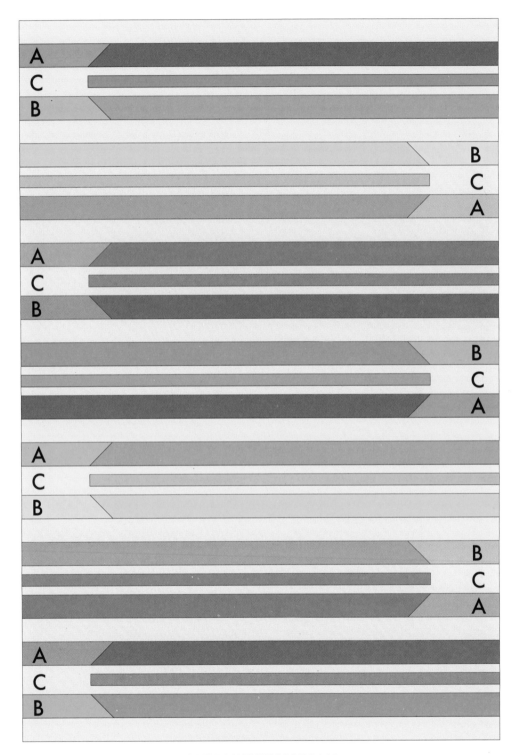

QUILT LAYOUT DIAGRAM

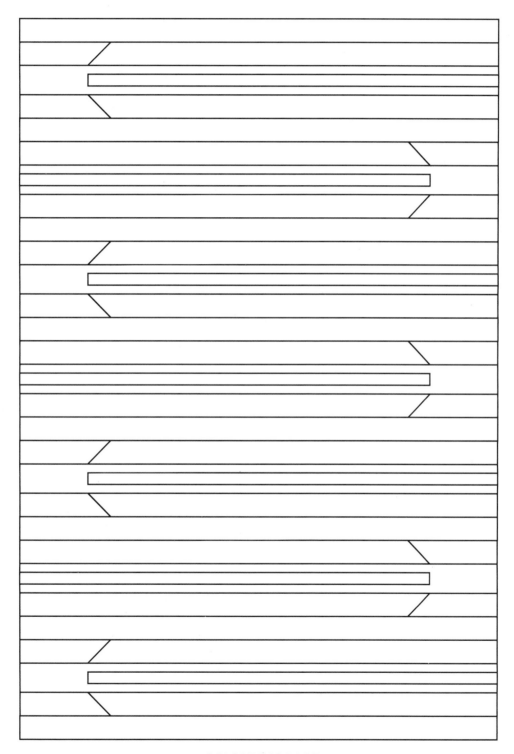

COLOURING PAGE

ombré compass double quilt

Sometimes the design comes first, and the fabric choice comes after, but sometimes you see a fabric and just have to design a quilt for it, like this one. I used Moda Ombré Confetti fabric, as it has Dark, Medium and Light areas, across the width, so I achieved all of my shades from the one ½ Yard piece per colour. If you are using non-Ombré fabric, then you will need to get a fat quarter of each of the three shades in each colour.

Size: 78" x 78"

Quilt Top Fabric:
- ½ Yard (½ m) Ombre fabric in Pink, Red, Orange, Yellow, Green, Blue-Green, Blue and Purple
- 3¾ Yards (3½m) White background

Finishing fabric:
- ¾ Yard (¾m- Binding fabric
- 5 Yards (4¾m) Backing fabric
- 84" x 84" (2.2m x 2.2m) square wadding

CUTTING INSTRUCTIONS

From each of the Pink, Orange, Green and Blue fabrics, cut;
(x4) 7¼" squares from the Dark shade area
(x4) 7¼" squares from the mid shade area
(x2) 7¼" strips from the Light shade area

From each of the Red, Yellow, Green-Blue and Purple fabrics, cut;
(x3) 7¼" squares from the Dark shade area
(x3) 7¼" squares from the Light shade area

From the White background fabric, cut;
(x23) 3⅞" WOF strips, sub cut in to (x224) 3⅞" squares
(x2) 7¼" WOF strips, sub cut in to (x8) 7¼" squares
(x4) 6½" WOF strips, sub cut in to (x20) 6½" squares
(x1) 12½" square

From the Binding fabric, cut;
(x8) 2½" WOF Strips

UNITS TO PREPARE

There are two types of units used in the quilt; Flying Geese (FG) and Half Square Triangles (HST).

FLYING GEESE

The finished size of the Flying Geese units is 3" x 6" (3½" x 6½" unfinished), made by using the no waste, four at a time method of Flying Geese on page 25.

STEP 1 Make the following FG units, using the 7 ¼" colour squares and the 3⅞" White squares.

Dark Shade Flying Geese:
(x8) Dark-Pink / White background

Block A. Corner Block

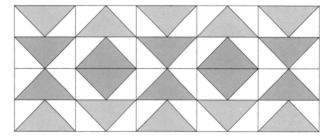

Block B. Joining Block

(x10) Dark-Red / White background
(x8) Dark-Orange / White background
(x10) Dark-Yellow / White background
(x8) Dark-Green / White background
(x10) Dark-Green-Blue / White background
(x8) Dark-Blue / White background
(x10) Dark-Purple / White background
Medium Shade Flying Geese:
(x16) Medium-Pink / White background
(x16) Medium-Orange / White background
(x16) Medium-Green / White background
(x16) Medium-Blue / White background
Light Shade Flying Geese:
(x8) Light-Pink / White background
(x10) Light-Red / White background
(x8) Light-Orange / White background
(x10) Light-Yellow / White background
(x8) Light-Green / White background
(x10) Light-Green-Blue / White background
(x8) Light-Blue / White background
(x10) Light-Purple / White background

HALF SQUARE TRIANGLES

The finished size of the HSTs is 6", remember this means you need to trim them to 6½" (unfinished). You

will use 7¼" squares to make the HST's using the two at a time method on page 22.

STEP 2 Make the following combinations and quantities of HSTs:
(x4) Dark-Pink / White background
(x4) Dark-Orange / White background
(x4) Dark-Green / White background
(x4) Dark-Blue / White background

QUILT BLOCKS

There are two main blocks in the quilt, Block A and Block B plus a White centre square.
Block A is the corner block and uses Dark, Medium and Light shades. Block A is constructed in four colour ways: Pink, Orange, Green and Blue.
Block B is the joining block and uses Dark and Light shades. Block B is constructed in four colour ways: Red, Yellow, Green-Blue and Purple.

CREATING THE CORNER BLOCKS (A)

STEP 3 Starting with the Pink corner block; sew together, along the long edge, two Light-Pink Flying Geese (FGs), so that they are pointing in the same direction. Make (x4) of these pairs.

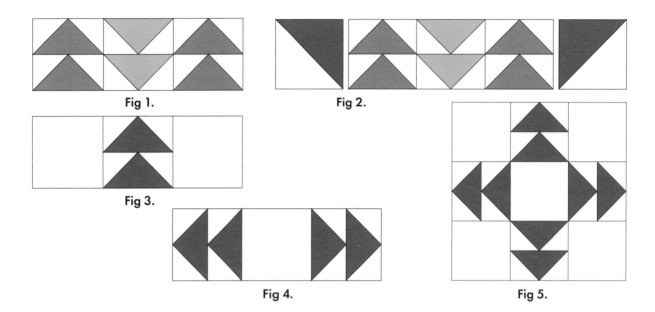

Fig 1.

Fig 2.

Fig 3.

Fig 4.

Fig 5.

STEP 4 Sew together, along the long edge, two Medium-Pink FGs so that they are pointing in the same direction, make (x8) of these pairs.

STEP 5 Sew together, along the long edge, two Dark-Pink FGs so that they are pointing in the same direction, make (x4) of these pairs.

STEP 6 Join (x2) pairs of Medium Pink FGs with (x1) pair of Light-Pink FGs, facing in the opposite direction in the middle. Make (x4) of these rows. (Fig 1)

STEP 7 Take (x2) of the rows you sewed in STEP 6 and add a Dark-Pink HST to each end of the row. Use Figure 2 as a guide for how to place the HSTs. (Fig 2)

STEP 8 Take (x2) pairs of the Dark-Pink FGs and add a 6½" White background square to each side. Make (x2) of these rows. (Fig 3)

STEP 9 Using the (x2) remaining pairs of Dark-Pink FGs join them together with a 6½" White square in the middle. (Fig 4)

STEP 10 Join the (x2) rows made in STEP 8 and the row made in STEP 9 to create the centre compass design. (Fig 5)

STEP 11 Sew on (x2) of the Light and Medium rows made in STEP 6 to the sides of the compass blocks (Fig 6) and then add the (x2) rows made in STEP 7 to the top and bottom of the compass block. (Fig 6)

STEP 12 Repeat the steps above in the remaining corner colours, Orange, Green and Blue; so that you have your four corner blocks.

CREATING THE JOINING BLOCKS (B)

STEP 13 Making sure that the Dark colour is at the top and they are pointing in the same direction; sew together, along the long edge, a Light-Yellow and Dark-Yellow FG. Make (x6) of these pairs.

STEP 14 Making sure the Light colour is at the top, and they are pointing in the same direction; sew together, along the long edge, a Light-Yellow and Dark-Yellow FG. Make (x4) of these pairs.

STEP 15 Take (x2) of the pairs made in STEP 13 and sew together so that they are facing each other, use (Fig 7) as a guide. Make (x3) of these rows.

STEP 16 Take (x2) of the pairs made in STEP 14 and sew together so they create a Dark square in the middle, use (Fig 8) as a guide. Make (x2) of these rows.

STEP 17 Join together the rows so that they create joining block (Fig 9).

PUTTING THE TOP TOGETHER

STEP 18 Using the layout diagram as a guide, sew the

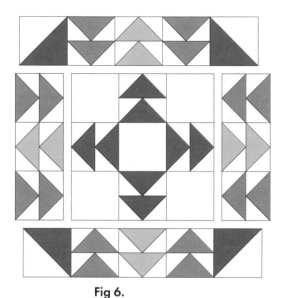

Fig 6.

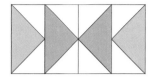

Fig 7.

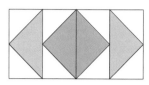

Fig 8.

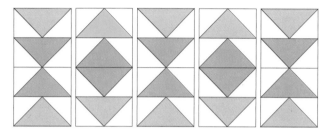

Fig 9.

Pink corner block with the Red centre block to the right; add the Orange corner block to the right to finish the top row.

STEP 19 Sew the Purple centre block, to the left-hand side of the 12½" White background square and the Yellow centre block to the right of the White square.

STEP 20 For row 3, sew together the Blue corner block with the Green-Blue centre block, Add the Green corner block to finish the bottom row.

STEP 21 Press the seams open and then sew together the three rows to complete the main top.

ADDING A BORDER

STEP 22 Taking the (x8) 3 ½" White background strips, join them together in pairs at a 45-degree angle, in the same way you join binding strips, to create four separate long strips.

STEP 23 Using a ¼" seam sew a border strip on to the top and bottom of the quilt top. Trim away any excess fabric and iron the seam open.

STEP 24 Using a ¼" seam sew a border strip on to the left- and right-hand sides of the quilt top. Trim away any excess fabric and iron open the seams.

FINISHING THE QUILT

STEP 25 If using normal width quilting cotton (approx. 44") you will need to cut a 5 Yard piece of fabric in half, creating (x2) 2½ Yard-long pieces. Cut away the selvedge and then join the two pieces together with a ½ in seam.

STEP 26 Give the backing fabric and quilt top a good press. Create a quilt sandwich and baste using your preferred method.

STEP 27 Quilt as desired, I chose to get this one professionally long arm quilted, but equally you could do some simple straight-line quilting diagonally across the quilt. If you are a free motion fan, then I'm sure there are lots of exciting ways to enhance the compass design.

STEP 28 Join your binding strips together using a 45-degree angle and then attach to the quilt. See the binding tutorial for help if needed.

ALTERNATIVES

If you don't have Ombre fabrics, you can create the effect by using different shades of the same colour. If you like a scrappy quilt you could make each section using all of the scraps you have in that colour.

QUILT LAYOUT DIAGRAM

COLOURING PAGE

starburst lap quilt

This quilt uses eight colours, in two shades, a Light and a Dark. I chose to use two background fabrics for extra detail. I used some of the wonderful Alison Glass Sun Print collections as they have such a variety of colours and shades available.

Size: 60" x 60"

Quilt Top Fabric:
- ◼ FQ each – Dark-Orange, Dark-Green, Dark-Blue and Dark-Pink

- ◼ FQ each – Light-Orange, Light-Green, Light-Blue and Light Pink

- ◼ FQ each – Dark-Yellow, Dark-Green-Blue, Dark-Purple and Dark-Red

- ◼ F8 each – Light-Yellow, Light-Green-Blue, Light-Purple and Light-Red

- ◼ 1 ½ yards (1 ½ m)- White background

- ◼ 1 ¼ Yards (1 ¼ m) - Grey background

Finishing Fabric:
- ◼ ¾ Yard (¾m) Binding Fabric

- ◼ 4 Yards (3¾m) Backing Fabric

- ◼ Wadding 66" (1.7m) square

CUTTING INSTRUCTIONS

From each of the Dark-Orange, Dark-Green, Dark-Blue and Dark-Pink fabrics, cut;
(x4) 6¼" squares
(x2) 5½" squares

From each of the Light-Orange, Light-Green, Light-Blue and Light-Pink fabrics, cut;
(x6) 6¼" Squares

From each of the Dark-Yellow, Dark-Green-Blue, Dark-Purple and Dark-Red fabrics, cut;
(x5) 6¼" Squares

From each of the Light-Yellow, Light-Green-Blue, Light-Purple and Light-Red fabrics, cut;
(x1) 6¼" Squares

From the main White background fabric, cut;
(x5) 6¼" WOF Strips, cut a total of (x28) 6 ¼" squares
(x3) 5½" WOF Strips, cut a total of (x16) 5 ½" squares

From the main Grey background fabric, cut;
(x5) 6¼" WOF Strips, cut a total of (x28) 6¼" squares
(x1) 5½" WOF Strips, cut a total of (x4) 5½" squares

From the binding fabric, cut;
(x7) 2½" WOF Strips

BLOCKS TO PREPARE
This quilt is made entirely from Half Square Triangles (HSTs) and squares.

HALF SQUARE TRIANGLES
Using the 6¼" squares, make the following HSTs, using the 2 at a time method on page 22:

STEP 1 Using the White background 6¼" squares make the following HST combinations:

(x2) Dark-Orange / White background
(x2) Dark-Green / White background
(x2) Dark-Blue / White background
(x2) Dark-Pink / White background
(x4) Light-Orange / White background
(x4) Light-Green / White background
(x4) Light-Blue / White background
(x4) Light-Pink / White background
(x6) Dark-Yellow / White background
(x6) Dark-Green-Blue / White background
(x6) Dark-Purple / White background
(x6) Dark-Red / White background
(x2) Light-Yellow / White background
(x2) Light-Green-Blue / White background
(x2) Light-Purple / White background
(x2) Light-Red / White background

STEP 2 Using the Grey background 6¼" squares make the following HST combinations:
(x3) Dark-Orange / Grey background
(x3) Dark-Green / Grey background
(x3) Dark-Blue / Grey background
(x3) Dark-Pink / Grey background
(x6) Light-Orange / Grey background
(x6) Light-Green / Grey background
(x6) Light-Blue / Grey background
(x6) Light-Pink / Grey background
(x4) Dark-Yellow / Grey background
(x4) Dark-Green-Blue / Grey background
(x4) Dark-Purple / Grey background
(x4) Dark-Red/ Grey background

STEP 3 Mixing the colour 6¼" squares make the following HST combinations:
(x2) Dark-Orange / Light-Orange
(x2) Dark-Green / Light-Green
(x2) Dark-Blue / Light-Blue
(x2) Dark-Pink / Light-Pink

STEP 4 Trim all of the HSTs made to 5½"

PUTTING THE TOP TOGETHER

Although this quilt looks like a complicated design it is relatively easy to put together as it is a combination of squares and HSTs, which are sewn together in rows.

STEP 5 Layout the squares in the order shown in the layout diagram, I find it useful to lay them out on the floor and take a photo once I have it right.

STEP 6 Collect up your squares in rows, labelling each row. I use a binding clip to keep each row separate and labelled.

STEP 7 Start with row 1 and sew together the squares using a ¼" seam. Continue on until you have sewn all twelve rows.

STEP 8 Iron Row 1 seams to the right-hand side. Iron the seams of Row 2 towards the left-hand side. Continue ironing the even numbered rows to the left and the odd numbered rows to the right. This will help when sewing the rows together.

STEP 9 Sew Rows 1 and 2 together, matching up and nestling the seams. Continue adding a row at a time.

FINISHING YOUR QUILT

STEP 10 If using normal width quilting cotton (approx. 44") you will need to cut a 4 Yard piece of fabric in half, creating (x2) 2-yard-long pieces. Cut away the selvedge and then join the two pieces together with a ½" seam. Iron open the seam.

STEP 11 Give the backing fabric and quilt top a good press and then baste using your preferred method.

STEP 12 Quilt as desired, I kept the quilting fairly simple with my usual 'go to' straight lines. To accentuate the star shape, I first straight line quilted diagonally across the quilt in the darker areas, once from top left to bottom right and then top right to bottom left. I finished by shadowing the V shapes left in between my diagonal quilting.

STEP 13 Join your binding strips together using a 45-degree angle and then attach to the quilt. See the binding tutorial for help if needed.

QUILT LAYOUT DIAGRAM

COLOURING PAGE

You can of course change the colour scheme to suit. I think a monochrome
version with a splash of colour would look great.

80s revival single quilt

I'm a child of the 80's so I love all things neon and bright. I wanted to create a quilt that took me back to my childhood of neon bracelets, plastic necklaces and spiky hair. The seven-colour rainbow doesn't quite work with this design, so I adapted it to six colours, leaving out the Purple, but adapt it your own way.

Size: 60" x 84"

Quilt Top Fabric:
- FQ each Plain Fabric in Pink, Red, Orange, Yellow, Green and Blue
- Long FQ of Pattern Fabric in Neon Pink, Neon Yellow and Neon Blue
- 2 Yards (2m) White Background
- ⅔ Yard (0.65m) Cream Background
- 1 Yard (1m) Black on White Sprinkles
- ½ Yard (½m) Black Fabric A
- ¾ Yard (¾m) Black Fabric B
- ½ Yard (½m) B&W Stripes

Finishing Fabric:
- ¾ Yard (¾m) Binding fabric
- 5 Yards (4 ¾m) Backing fabric
- 65" x 90" (1.65m x 2.3m) wadding

CUTTING INSTRUCTIONS

From each of the six plain fabrics, cut;
(x2) 7¼" squares
(x8) 3⅞" squares

From each of the three patterned Neon colours, cut;
(x5) 8" squares

From White background fabric, cut;
(x3) 7¼" WOF strips, sub cut into a total of (x14) 7¼" squares
(x6) 8" WOF strips, sub cut into a total of (x27) 8" squares

From Cream background fabric, cut;
(x5) 3⅞" WOF strips, sub cut into a total of (x48) 3⅞" squares

From Black on White sprinkles fabric, cut;
(x2) 4¾" WOF strips, sub cut into a total of (x12) 4¾" squares
(x8) 3⅞" squares
(x3) 8" squares
(x2) 3½" WOF strips, sub cut into a total of (x6) 12½" x 3½" rectangles

From Black fabric A, cut;
(x3) 3⅞" WOF strips, sub cut into a total of (x24) 3⅞" squares

From Black fabric B, cut;
(x3) 8" WOF strips, sub cut into a total of (x15) 8" squares

From the Black & White stripes fabric, cut;
(x5) 3½" WOF strips

From the Binding fabric, cut;
(x8) 2½" WOF strips

UNITS TO PREPARE

The quilt is made up of Flying Geese (FG), Half Square Triangles (HST) and Diamonds in Squares (DS).

FLYING GEESE

The Flying Geese units in the blocks use the four at a time method described in the tutorials page 26. The centre 'geese' parts of the unit

are made from a 7¼" square and the smaller corner 'sky' triangles are made from (x4) 3⅞" squares. Remember for each large square and four small square combination you will get four Flying Geese. So, if you need eight Flying Geese then follow the method two times.

STEP 1 where the white background fabric is the large 7¼" square and the six plain colours are the smaller 3⅞" squares. Make the following Flying Geese combinations:
(x8) White background / Pink
(x8) White background / Red
(x8) White background / Orange
(x8) White background / Yellow
(x8) White background / Green
(x8) White background / Blue

STEP 2 where the six plain colour fabrics are the large 7¼" squares and the cream background fabric is the smaller 3⅞" squares. Make the following Flying Geese combinations:
(x8) Pink / cream background
(x8) Red / cream background
(x8) Orange / cream background
(x8) Yellow / cream background
(x8) Green / cream background
(x8) Blue / cream background

STEP 3 Where the white background fabric is the large 7¼" square and the Black on White sprinkles fabric is the smaller 3⅞" squares. Make (x6) Flying Geese units.

(note you will have two spare fg units as you are using the four at a time method twice).

HALF SQUARE TRIANGLES
The Half Square Triangle (HST) units in the blocks use the eight at a time method described in the tutorials

page 24. The starting squares are 8" and this will give you eight HSTs which each need to be trimmed to 3½". Remember for each large square pair you will get eight HSTs. So, if you need thirty-six HSTs then follow the method five times.

STEP 4 Make the following combinations and quantities of HSTs:
(x36) Neon Pink / White background
(x36) Neon Yellow / White background
(x36) Neon Blue / White background
(x96) Black fabric B / White background
(x24) Black fabric B / Black on White sprinkles fabric

DIAMOND IN A SQUARE
The Diamond in Square units are made with one 4¾" Black on White sprinkles square in the centre and four Black fabric A triangles, cut from two 3⅞" squares.

STEP 5 Follow the instructions in the tutorial page 27 to make (x12) Diamond in Square units. Each will measure 6½" square (unfinished size).

QUILT BLOCKS
There are two main quilt blocks; a part block plus a full block. Each block appears in the following three colour ways:
1) Red, Pink and Neon Pink
2) Blue, Green and Neon Blue
3) Yellow, Orange and Neon Yellow

CREATING THE PART BLOCKS
STEP 6 Sew together a Neon Pink/White HST with a Black B/Black on White sprinkles HST following the layout in (Fig 1).
STEP 7 Sew together another Neon Pink/White HST with a Black B/Black on White sprinkles HST following the layout in (Fig 2). This is the mirror image of the pair in STEP 6.
STEP 8 Sew a White background/Black on White

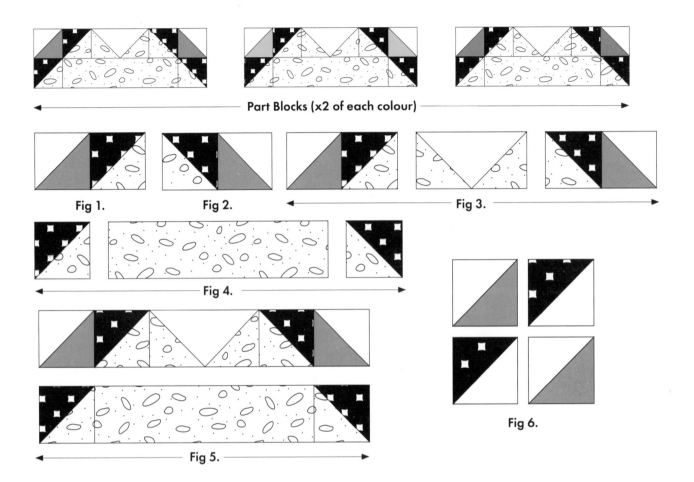

Part Blocks (x2 of each colour)

Fig 1. Fig 2. Fig 3.

Fig 4.

Fig 5.

Fig 6.

sprinkles Flying Geese unit in between the two HST pairs created above, following the layout in (Fig 3).

STEP 9 Take the Black on White sprinkles 12½" x 3½" rectangle and sew a Black B/ Black on White sprinkles HST at either side, following the layout in (Fig 4).

STEP 10 Sew together the two rows created in STEPS 8 & 9, following the layout in (Fig 5).

STEP 11 Repeat steps above to create a total of (x2) part blocks per colour way, by changing Pink Neon HSTs for Neon Yellow HSTs and Neon Blue HSTs.

CREATING THE FULL BLOCKS

STEP 12 Sew together two Pink/White background HSTs with two Black B/White HSTs to create the block in (Fig 6). Make four (x4) of these.

STEP 13 Sew together a White/Pink FG unit with a Neon Pink/Cream FG unit to create the arrow shape

in (Fig 7). Make two (x2) of these.

STEP 14 Repeat STEP 13 with the Red Flying Geese units (Fig 8). Make (x2) of these.

STEP 15 Join together two of the corner blocks from STEP 12 with a Pink Flying Geese pair in the middle facing down. (Fig 9)

STEP 16 Join together the two remaining corner blocks from STEP 12 with a Red Flying Geese pair in the middle facing upwards.

STEP 17 Take a diamond in square unit and add a Pink Flying Geese pair to the left-hand side pointing inwards. Add a Red Flying Geese pair to the right-hand side facing inwards. (Fig 10)

STEP 18 Take the three rows and join them together to create the block in (Fig 11).

STEP 19 Repeat STEPS 12 to 18 to create a total of four quilt blocks in each colour way.

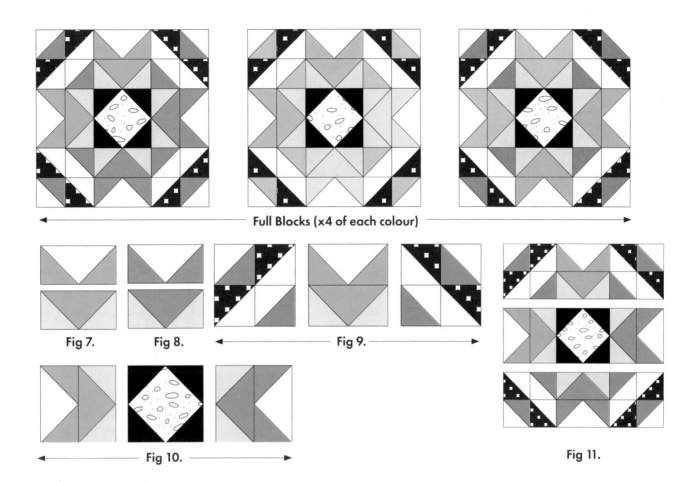

Full Blocks (x4 of each colour)

Fig 7.   Fig 8.   Fig 9.

Fig 10.

Fig 11.

PUTTING THE TOP TOGETHER

STEP 20 Sew the blocks together in rows, following the layout diagram. Once you have sewn each row, sew them together to create the top.

STEP 21 Prepare the Black and White striped piece by sewing together the (x5) 3½" WOF strips, then cutting it in half. Sew one half to the left side and one side to the right side. Trim off any excess fabric and your top is complete.

FINISHING THE QUILT

STEP 22 If using regular width quilting cotton (approx. 44") you will need to cut a 5 Yard piece of fabric in half, creating two (x2) 2½ Yard long pieces. Join the two pieces together with a ½" seam, cut away the selvedge and press open the seam.

STEP 23 Give the backing fabric and quilt top a good press. Create a quilt sandwich and baste using your preferred method.

STEP 24 Quilt as desired, I chose to get this one professionally long arm quilted, with some wavy lines running up the length of the quilt. You could do some simple straight lines across the width of the quilt instead.

STEP 25 Join your binding strips together using a 45-degree angle and then attach to the quilt. See the binding tutorial for help if needed.

ALTERNATIVES

Change the colour scheme to suit. I designed the quilt to be a single bed quilt. If you want to make it fit a larger double bed, then add an extra column of blocks down the side, before attaching the Black and White strips.

QUILT LAYOUT DIAGRAM

COLOURING PAGE

picnic squares quilt

*This quilt works well with eight rainbow colours and two background colours.
I used the seven standard rainbow colours and added in a Green-Blue fabric.
Make sure your two background fabrics contrast so the grid stands out.*

Size: 51" x 51"

Quilt Top Fabric:
- FQ Red, Orange, Yellow, Green, Blue, Blue-Green, Purple and Pink
- 1¼ Yards (1m) Light-Grey background
- ⅔ Yard (0.65m) Low volume background

Finishing Fabric:
- ½ Yard (½m) Binding fabric
- 2 Yards (1.85m) Backing fabric
- 50" (1.3m) square wadding

CUTTING INSTRUCTIONS

From each of the eight colour fabrics, cut;
(x3) 3½" Fat quarter strips

From the Low volume background fabric, cut;
(x3) 3½" WOF Strips, sub cut (x2) strips in half giving you (x4) 21" strips.
(x3) 3½" WOF Strips, sub cut into (x12) 3½" x 9½" rectangles

From the Light-Grey background fabric, cut;
(x9) 3½" WOF Strips, sub cut (x1) strip in half giving you (x2) 21" strips.
(x2) 3½" WOF Strips, sub cut into (x8) 3½" x 9½" rectangles

QUILT BLOCKS

The quilt is made from nine-patch blocks, sewn together from strips.
There are three types of blocks.

Blocks A - Rainbow Colour block
Blocks B - Cross background blocks
Blocks C - T-shape background blocks

CREATING BLOCK A

You need to make a total of (x13) rainbow Block As. The nine-patches are created by sewing together the 3½" strips of fabric first.

STEP 1 Create the strips for each of the three colour ways below, by sewing three strips together along the long edge in the order stated. Once sewn cut a total of (x13) 3½" wide slices, from each colour way. (Fig 1)
(x3) Strip 1 – Red, Orange, Yellow
(x3) Strip 2 - Pink, Low volume background, Green
(x3) Strip 3 – Purple, Blue, Blue-Green

STEP 2 Iron the seams of the Red to Yellow slice and the Purple to Green-Blue slice to the right. Iron the Pink to Green slice to the left. This will help match up the seams when you sew them together.

STEP 3 Sew together the three different slices to create the nine-patch. (Fig 2)

STEP 4 Repeat giving you (x13) rainbow nine patches.

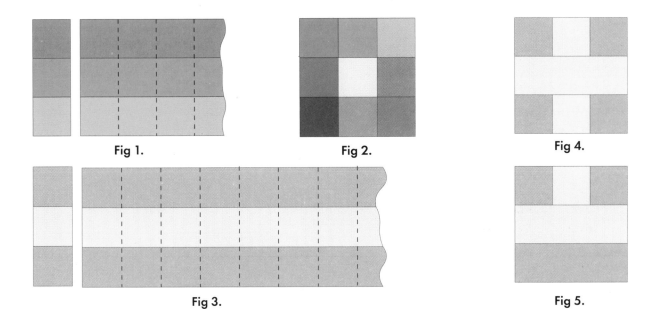

Fig 1.

Fig 2.

Fig 4.

Fig 3.

Fig 5.

CREATING BLOCK B

STEP 5 Sew together (x2) 3½" WOF strips of Light-Grey background fabric with (x1) 3½" WOF of Low volume fabric placed in the middle. Cut the strip into (x12) 3½" wide slices. (Fig 3)

STEP 6 Repeat with the 21" x 3½" strips and cut into (x4) 3½" slices, giving you a total of (x16) 3½" slices.

STEP 7 Sew together (x2) of the slices from STEP 6, with a Low volume 3½" x 9½" rectangle in the middle. Repeat so that you have (x4) of these blocks. (Fig 4)

CREATING BLOCK C

STEP 8 Sew together (x1) Light-Grey 3½" x 9½" rectangle, (x1) 3½" x 9½" Low volume background rectangle and one of the slices from STEP 6. Repeat so that you have (x8) of these blocks. (Fig 5)

PUTTING THE TOP TOGETHER

STEP 9 Following the layout diagram sew together the blocks into the five rows shown.

STEP 10 Sew the rows together, to complete the centre.

STEP 11 Take two of the 3½" Grey WOF border strips and cut in half. Sew each of these halves to one of the full strips, using a 45-degree angle. You now have 4 long border pieces.

STEP 12 Sew a border piece to the left- and right-hand sides and then trim away any excess fabric. Finish by sewing the remaining strips to the top and bottom and trimming away the excess.

FINISHING YOUR QUILT

STEP 13 If using normal width quilting cotton (approx. 44") you will need to cut a 3¼ Yard piece of fabric in half, creating (x2) 1⅞ Yard-long pieces. Cut away the selvedge and then join the two pieces together with a ½" seam. Iron open the seam.

STEP 14 Give the backing fabric and quilt top a good press and baste using your preferred method.

STEP 15 I used straight line quilting to shadow the nine-patches, giving it a checked quilting design.

STEP 16 Join your binding strips together using a 45-degree angle and then attach to the quilt. See the binding tutorial for help, if needed.

ALTERNATIVES

You can, of course, change the colour scheme to suit, or use some fun child prints so you can have a game of eye-spy whilst having a picnic. You can also use waterproof fabric on the underside. There are some tips on my website, if you fancy giving this a go.

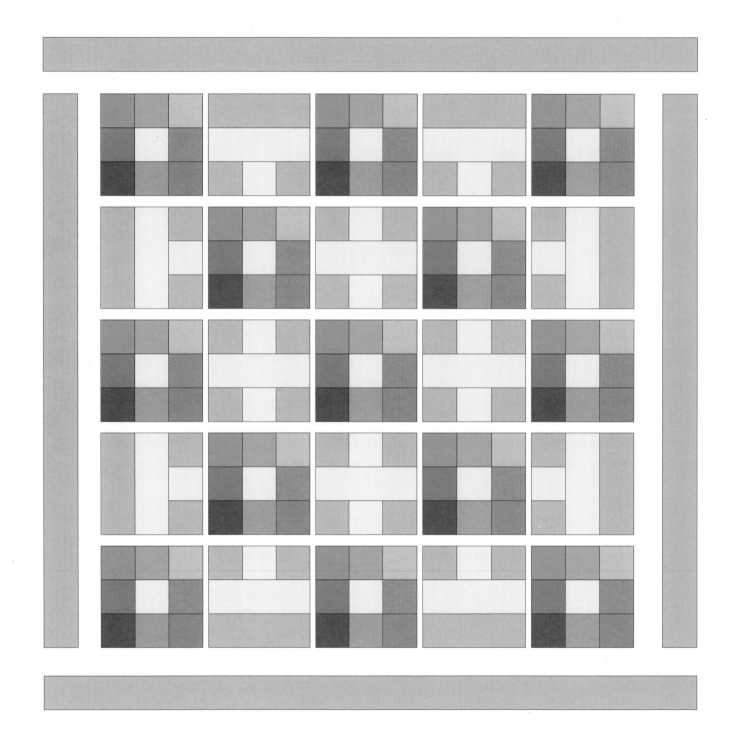

QUILT LAYOUT DIAGRAM

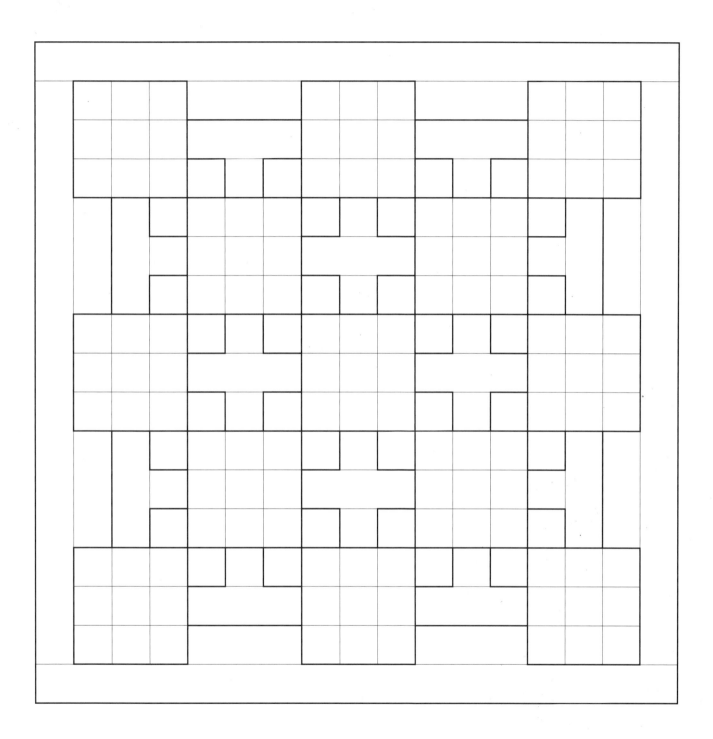

COLOURING PAGE

chapter four: cushion projects

Cushions are a great way to hone your new skills. They are quicker to make than quilts, fit easily under your sewing machine and you can use up of any scraps and small pieces of fabric that you have left over from other projects. You will find five cushion projects in this section, so you should find something fun to make when you don't have the time for a quilt project. I find them very useful for trying out new designs...

vintage dash cushion

I wanted the cushion to match the Vintage Star quilt, so used a lot of the same fabrics. Patterned fabrics give it a scrappy look. Go to town with your scraps for this cushion! They are small HSTs, so easy to make from small pieces of fabric.

Size: 28" x 18"

Cushion Top Fabric:
- 1 F8 each of 'bright' - Red, Yellow, Green-Blue, Purple
- 1 F8 each of 'bright'- Orange, Green, Blue and Pink
- 1 F8 each of 'Low volume'- Red, Orange, Yellow, Green, Green-Blue, Blue, Purple and Pink
- F8 Black & White striped fabric
- 1 F8 Black fabric
- 1 F8 White fabric

Note: If you have made the Vintage Star quilt and saved the extra Half Square Triangles then you will not need to make the Half Square Triangles, you'll just need to trim them.

Cushion Fabric:
- 28" x 18" (72cm x 46cm) cushion inner or pillow
- ½ yard (½m) for the cushion back
- F8 Binding fabric
- 30" x 20" (¾m x ½m) wadding rectangle
- (x2) 19½" (50cm) square wadding pieces
- 1 yard (1m)- optional inner fabric, such as calico

CUTTING INSTRUCTIONS

From each of the bright Red, Yellow, Green-Blue and Purple fabrics, cut;
(x3) 5" squares

From each of the bright Orange, Green, Blue and Pink fabrics, cut;
(x12) 2½" x 1½" rectangles

From the Low volume fabrics Red, Yellow, Green-Blue and Purple fabrics, cut;
(x3) 5" squares

From the Low volume fabrics Orange, Green, Blue and Pink fabrics, cut;
(x12) 2½" x 1½" rectangles

From the Black & White striped fabric, cut;
(x2) 2½" x 18½" strips

From the Black fabric, cut;
(x6) 2½" squares

From the White fabric, cut;
(x6) 2½" squares

From the cushion back fabric, cut;
(x2) 19½" squares

UNITS TO PREPARE

Half Square Triangles

The HSTs for this cushion are made using the four at a time HST method. To make the four HSTs match together 5" squares of the bright and Low volume fabrics. Skip to STEP 2 if you have your HSTs already.

STEP 1 Make the following HSTs in the following combinations:
(x12) Red / Low volume Red
(x12) Yellow / Low volume Yellow
(x12) Aqua / Low volume Green-Blue
(x12) Purple / Low volume Purple

STEP 2 Trim your HST units to 2½" (unfinished size)

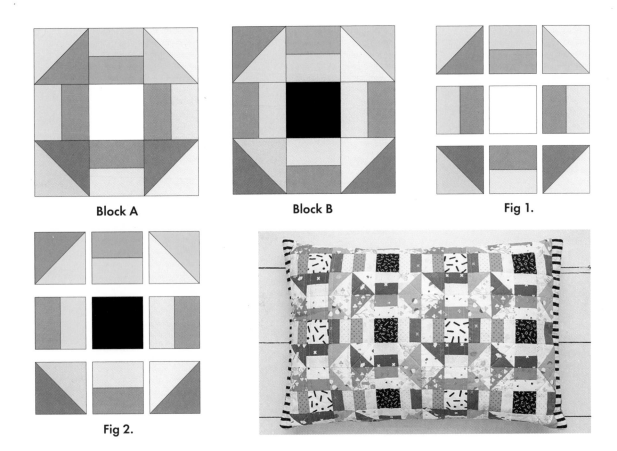

Block A

Block B

Fig 1.

Fig 2.

STEP 3 Make the striped units by matching up a 1½"
x 2½" bright rectangle and the corresponding Low
volume rectangle. Sew the rectangles together along
the long edge. Make the following combinations:
(x12) Orange / Low volume Orange
(x12) Green / Low volume Green
(x12) Blue / Low volume Blue
(x12) Pink / Low volume Pink

BLOCKS

Churn Dash blocks are made from (x4) HSTs and (x4)
striped blocks, plus a centre square. There are two
types, depending on how the units are rotated.
Block A with a light 'Low volume' background and
White centre square
Block B with a 'bright' colour background and black
centre square.

BLOCK A

STEP 4 To make the light background Churn Dash
Block set out the HSTs and striped blocks following
Block A layout.
STEP 5 Sew each row together, press the seams open.
Sew the three rows together to make the block. (Fig 1)
STEP 6 Repeat steps 4 and 5 so that you have a total
of (x6) A Blocks.

BLOCK B

STEP 7 To make the colour background Churn Dash
Block set out the HSTs and striped blocks following
Block B layout.
STEP 8 Sew each row together, iron the seams open.
Sew the three rows together to make the block. (Fig 2)
STEP 9 Repeat steps 7 and 8 so that you have a total
of (x6) B Blocks.

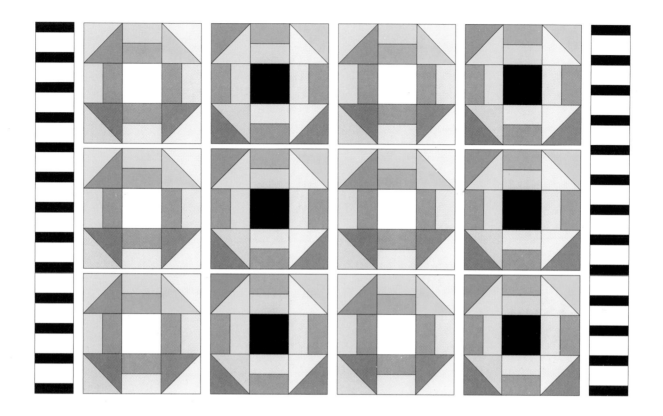

PUTTING THE TOP TOGETHER

STEP 10 Sew (x3) A blocks together in a vertical column, repeat so that you have (x2) of these.

STEP 11 Sew (x3) B Blocks together in a vertical column, repeat so that you have (x2) of these.

STEP 12 Sew the Block A and Block B columns together alternatively following the cushion layout diagram.

STEP 13 Take the (x2) 18½" x 2½" Black & White striped rectangles and sew one to each short side (left and right) of the cushion top.

QUILTING YOUR CUSHION

STEP 14 Place the cushion top onto your piece of wadding and use spray baste or basting pins to keep steady. Optionally you may like to add a backing fabric under the wadding, this will keep the inner of your cushion nice and neat.

STEP 15 Quilt the cushion top. I quilted straight lines down the Low volume columns and then diagonally across each of the bright Churn Dash blocks, to give some differentiation. Once quilted trim back the cushion to 18½" x 28½".

STEP 16 Layer each of the two 19½" square cushion backs with wadding and baste. You can add a fabric to the back of the wadding for the inner of the cushion.

STEP 17 Quilt the cushion back squares. Keep it simple by quilting straight lines diagonally across the backing fabrics. Once finished trim back to 18½" square.

STEP 18 Take a 2" x 18½" strip of binding fabric and fold it in half lengthways. Fold the long raw edges in to the centre of the strip and iron in place. You can use ready-made binding if you have some.

STEP 19 Add a strip of binding to one side of each of the quilted backing pieces by placing the quilted piece inside the binding strip and top stitching in place.

STEP 20 Use the envelope cushion tutorial to complete the cushion.

cabin blocks cushion

I used eight colours for the cabin block in this project. Each colour had a plain fabric and a spotted fabric to match. You could use bright and light shades of colours instead, as shown in the layout diagram.

Size: 18" x 18"

Quilt Top Fabric:
- 1 F8 each- plain fabric in Red, Orange, Yellow, Green, Green-Blue, Blue, Purple, Pink
- 1 F8 each- spotted fabric in Red, Orange, Yellow, Green, Green-Blue, Blue, Purple, Pink

Cushion Fabric:
- Cushion inner 18" (46cm) square
- ½ Yard (½m) - cushion back fabric
- 20" (½ m) square wadding
- 1 F8 Binding fabric
- ½ Yard (½ m) - optional inner fabric, such as calico

CUTTING INSTRUCTIONS

The cabin block is made from a starting 2" square and 1¼" strips of fabric, which increase in length as you move around the block. The table on page 82 gives the size of the strips, which correspond to the layout diagram of the cabin block. The spotted fabric is shown as the lighter colour.

Fig 1. Fig 2. Fig 3. Fig 4.

MAKING THE CUSHION TOP

TIP I find it useful to mark an arrow on the starting square pointing upwards to help me orientate the block as I am adding strips. Make sure you use a marker or sticker that you can remove afterwards though.

STEP 1 Take the 2" Red square (A) and sew the 1¼" x 2" (B) Orange spot strip to the top. Iron the seams towards the Orange spot (away from the square). (Fig 1)

STEP 2 Take the 1¼". x 2¾" (C) Orange spot piece and sew to the right-hand side of the block. Again, iron the seams out away from the square. (Fig 2)

STEP 3 Take the 1¼" x 2¾" (D) Orange strip and sew to the bottom of the block, again ironing the seams outwards. (Fig 3)

STEP 4 Take the 1¼" x 3½" (E) Orange strip and sew to the right-hand side of the block, iron seams out again. (Fig 4)

STEP 5 Continue adding the rows in order, going in a clock-wise direction, by sewing the top, then the right-hand side, then the bottom, and finally the left-hand side. Make sure you iron your seams outwards after sewing each strip. Use the table and layout diagram to keep on track of the fabrics and sizes.

A	2″ square	Red	**Q**	1¼″ x 8″	Aqua	**AG**	1¼″ x 14″	Red
B	1¼″ x 2″	Orange spot	**R**	1¼″ x 8″	Blue spot	**AH**	1¼″ x 14″	Orange spot
C	1¼″ x 2¾″	Orange spot	**S**	1¼″ x 8¾″	Blue spot	**AI**	1¼″ x 14¾″	Orange spot
D	1¼″ x 2¾″	Orange	**T**	1¼″ x 8¾″	Blue	**AJ**	1¼″ x 14¾″	Orange
E	1¼″ x 3½″	Orange	**U**	1¼″ x 9½″	Blue	**AK**	1¼″ x 15½″	Orange
F	1¼″ x 3½″	Yellow spot	**V**	1¼″ x 9½″	Purple spot	**AL**	1¼″ x 15½″	Yellow spot
G	1¼″ x 4¼″	Yellow spot	**W**	1¼″ x 10¼″	Purple spot	**AM**	1¼″ x 16¼″	Yellow spot
H	1¼″ x 4¼″	Yellow	**X**	1¼″ x 10¼″	Purple	**AN**	1¼″ x 16¼″	Yellow
I	1¼″ x 5″	Yellow	**Y**	1¼″ x 11″	Purple	**AO**	1¼″ x 17″	Yellow
J	1¼″ x 5″	Green spot	**Z**	1¼″ x 11″	Pink spot	**AP**	1¼″ x 17″	Green spot
K	1¼″ x 5¾″	Green spot	**AA**	1¼″ x 11¾″	Pink spot	**AQ**	1¼″ x 17¾″	Green spot
L	1¼″ x 5¾″	Green	**AB**	1¼″ x 11¾″	Pink	**AR**	1¼″ x 17¾″	Green
M	1¼″ x 6½″	Green	**AC**	1¼″ x 12½″	Pink	**AS**	1¼″ x 18½″	Green
N	1¼″ x 6½″	Aqua spot	**AD**	1¼″ x 12½″	Red spot			
O	1¼″ x 7¼″	Aqua spot	**AE**	1¼″ x 13¼″	Red spot			
P	1¼″ x 7¼″	Aqua	**AF**	1¼″ x 13¼″	Red			

CUTTING INSTRUCTIONS

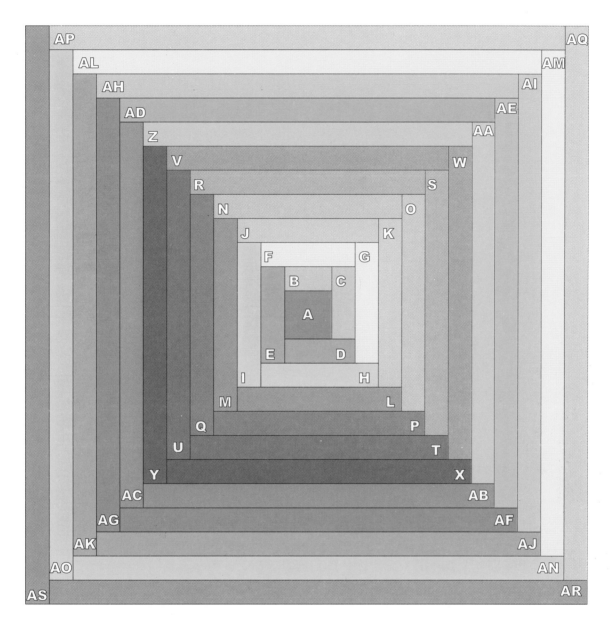

QUILTING YOUR CUSHION TOP

STEP 6 Place the quilt top on to your piece of wadding and use spray baste or basting pins to keep steady. Optionally you may like to add a backing fabric under the wadding, this will keep the inner of your cushion nice and neat.

STEP 7 Quilt the cushion top. I quilted with a sun burst design, using straight diagonal lines getting wider as they went out from the corner. Once quilted trim back to an 18½" square.

STEP 8 Cut (x2) 18½" x 13½" rectangles from your cushion back fabric.

STEP 9 Take a 2" x 18½" strip of binding fabric and fold it in half lengthways. Fold the long raw edges in to the centre of the strip and iron in place. You can use ready-made binding if you have some.

STEP 10 Add a strip of binding to one side of each of the backing pieces by placing the fabric inside the binding strip and top stitching in place.

STEP 11 Use the envelope cushion tutorial to finish.

shaded arrows cushion

I chose to re-use some of the Ombre confetti fabric used in the Ombre compass quilt. This cushion uses the gradient of the Ombre fabric and it looks fantastic - complementing the Ombre compass quilt or standing out as a standalone piece.

Size: 18" square

Cushion Top Fabric:
- F8 each of Pink, Yellow, Green, Green-Blue, Blue and Purple fabrics
- ½ yard (½m) of White background fabric
- F8 of binding fabric

Cushion Fabric:
- 18" (46cm) square - cushion inner
- ½ yard (½m) - cushion backing fabric
- 20" (½m) square wadding
- 1 yard (1m) - optional inner such as calico

CUTTING INSTRUCTIONS
From the White background fabric, cut;
(x18) 3½" x6 ½" rectangles
From each of the Pink, Yellow, Green, Green-Blue, Blue and Purple fabrics, cut;
(x6) 3½" squares
From the cushion backing fabric cut;
(x2) 18½" X 13½" rectangles
From the binding fabric cut;
(x2) 2" x 18½" strips

UNITS TO PREPARE
Flying Geese units
The Flying Geese units are created using the one at a time method. Each Flying Geese unit is made from (x1) White 6½" x 3½" rectangle and (x2) 3½" squares in different colours, one for the left and one for the right. I also used four different shades of each colour to give the gradient effect.

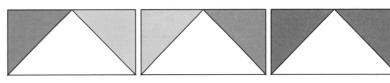

Fig 1.

STEP 1 Make the following Flying Geese in the following combinations, where the white fabric is the large rectangle and the colours are the small squares. (Fig 1)

(x6) Pink / White / Yellow
(x6) Green / White / Green-Blue
(x6) Blue / White / Purple

LAYOUT DIAGRAM

PUTTING THE TOP TOGETHER

STEP 2 Sew the (x6) Pink and Yellow Flying Geese units together in to a column. If you are using an Ombre effect fabric, then order them from light to dark.

STEP 3 Repeat with the Green and Green-Blue Flying Geese and the Blue and Purple Flying Geese.

STEP 4 Iron the seams of row 1 and 3 downwards and the seams of row 2 upwards, to nestle the seams together. Sew (x3) columns of Flying Geese together so Pink triangles are on the left and Purple triangles are on the right. Use the layout diagram as a guide.

QUILTING YOUR CUSHION TOP

STEP 5 Place the quilt top on to your piece of wadding and use spray baste or basting pins to keep steady. You may like to add a backing fabric under the wadding, which keeps the inner nice and neat.

STEP 6 Quilt the cushion top. I quilted straight lines in a

V shape to accentuate the Flying Geese shape. Once quilted trim back to an 18½" square.

STEP 7 Take the (x2) 18½" x 13½" cushion back fabrics, basting each piece to one of the 20½" x 15" pieces of wadding. If you like you can add a fabric to the back of the wadding for the inner of the cushion.

STEP 8 Quilt the cushion backs. Keep it simple by quilting straight lines diagonally across the backing fabrics. Once quilted trim each piece to 18½" x 13½".

STEP 9 Take a 2" x 18½" strip of binding fabric and fold it in half lengthways. Fold the long raw edges in to the centre of the strip and iron in place. You can use ready-made binding if you have some.

STEP 10 Add a strip of binding to one side of each of the quilted backing pieces by placing the quilted piece inside the binding strip and top stitching in place.

STEP 11 Use the envelope cushion tutorial to complete the cushion.

garden floor cushion

I wanted to echo the design of the Picnic quilt using some colourful fabrics I've been collecting. I chose fabrics with an outside theme: animals, weather and food. It makes for a great 'I-spy' game! The cushion uses eight colours plus a Grey centre square. Each colour has a patterned fabric, a Dark plain and a Light plain.

Size: 30" x 30"

Cushion Top Fabric:
- ▣ 1 F8 each- Patterned, Red, Orange, Yellow, Green, Green-Blue, Blue, Purple, Pink, and Grey fabrics

- ▣ 1 F8 each – Light plain, Red, Orange, Yellow, Green, Green-Blue, Blue, Purple, Pink, and Grey fabrics

- ▣ Scraps Dark plain Red, Orange, Yellow, Green, Green-Blue, Blue, Purple, Pink, and Grey fabrics

- ▣ 1 long FQ (¼m)- border fabric (S)

Cushion Fabric:
- ▣ 30" (77cm) square cushion inner

- ▣ 1½ Yards (1½m) cushion back fabric

- ▣ 34" x 34" (0.92m) square wadding

CUTTING INSTRUCTIONS

From each of the nine patterned fabrics, cut;
(x1) 7½" square

From each of the nine Light plain fabrics, cut;
(x4) 1½" x 7½" rectangles

From each of the nine Dark plain fabrics, cut;
(x4) 1½" squares

From the border fabric, cut;
(x2) 2" x 27½" strips
(x2) 2" x 30½" strips

BLOCKS

Each block is made by framing the centre square. If you have some fabrics with great patterns you could fussy cut the squares. I used animal-and-food-themed fabrics.

BLOCK A

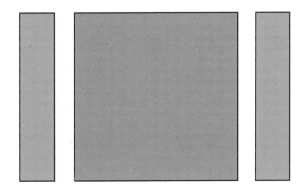

Fig 1.

STEP 1 Take the Red patterned 7½" square and sew a Light Red 1½" x 7½" rectangle to the right- and left-hand sides. (Fig 1)

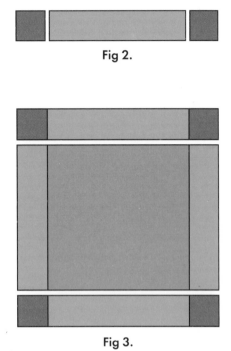

Fig 2.

Fig 3.

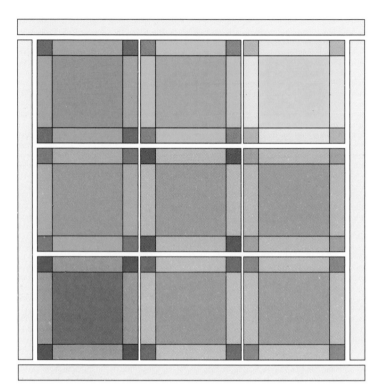

LAYOUT DIAGRAM

STEP 2 Sew a Dark Red 1½" square to either end of the (x2) plain Light Red 7½" x 1½" rectangles not sewn on to the main square. Iron open the seams. (Fig 2)

STEP 3 Sew the two Red strips sewn in STEP 2 to the top and bottom of the Red square. (Fig 3)

STEP 4 Repeat the above steps so that you have one framed square for each of the eight colours plus the Grey one.

PUTTING THE CUSHION TOP TOGETHER

STEP 5 Sew nine blocks together by sewing the squares into three rows pressing the seams for rows 1 and 3 to the right and row 2 to the left. Match up the seams and then sew the rows together. (layout diagram)

STEP 6 Iron the seams nice and flat and then sew on the (x2) 2" x 27½" strips, one to the left and one to the right side. Iron the seams open.

STEP 7 Finish the border by sewing the remaining (x2) border strips to the top and bottom of the cushion top.

QUILTING YOUR CUSHION TOP

STEP 8 Place the quilt top onto your piece of wadding and use spray baste or basting pins to keep steady. Optionally you may like to add a backing fabric under the wadding, this will keep the inner of your cushion nice and neat.

STEP 9 Quilt the cushion top. I quilted within each of the squares and then added straight lines around the framed areas. Once quilted, trim back to a 30½" square.

STEP 10 Take your two backing pieces 30½" x 20" and hem the one of the long edges on each piece. To hem the piece, simply turn the fabric over ½" then turn over again and top stitch in place.

STEP 11 Use the envelope cushion tutorial to complete the cushion.

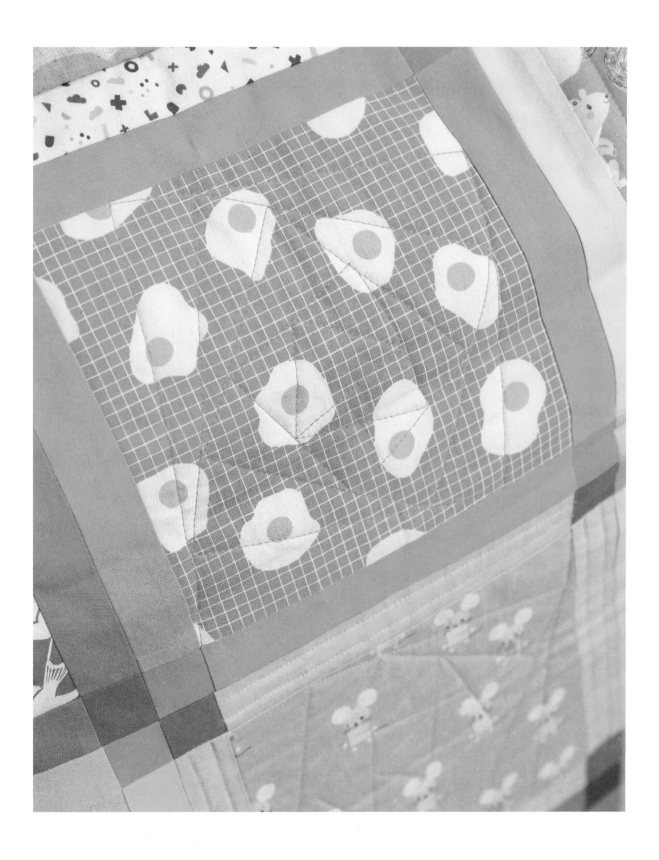

neon squares cushion

This cushion is a really quick make and simple to put together. You can experiment with lots of different fabrics, it doesn't have to be neon. I chose to use some of the same neon fabrics from the 80s revival quilt, plus a few extra Low volume background prints. It's defiinitely one of my favourite designs.

Size: 18" square

Cushion Top Fabric:
- F8 – each of Pink, Red, Orange, Yellow, Green and Blue
- F8 – each of (x3) different Low volume prints
- F8 – Low volume Centre strip print

Cushion Fabric:
- 18" (46cm) square cushion inner
- ½ Yard (½m) for the cushion back
- 20" (½m) square wadding
- 1 Yard (1m) - optional inner fabric such as calico

CUTTING INSTRUCTIONS

From each of the Pink, Red, Orange, Yellow, Green and Blue fabrics, cut;
(x2) 1¼" x 18" strips

From each of the three Low volume prints, cut;
(x4) 1½" x 18" strips

From the Low volume centre strip fabric, cut:
(x6) 1½" x 18" strips

From the cushion backing fabric, cut;
(x2) 18½" x 14½"

PUTTING THE TOP TOGETHER

The squares are created by cutting slices from a sewn strip. Each strip is created from (x5) fabrics; a Low volume centre strip, two colours and two strips of a matching Low volume fabric. The 18" strips of fabric are longer than you need, so there is room for error.

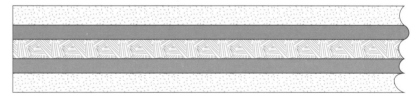

Fig 1.

STEP 1 Sew together the centre Low volume strip with a red or pink strip on each side. Next, add a Low volume strip to the opposite sides of the colour strips. (Fig 1)

STEP 2 Repeat so that you have (x2) strips for the following combinations:
Low volume 1 - Red - Centre fabric – Pink - Low volume 1
Low volume 2 – Orange - Centre fabric – Yellow - Low volume 2
Low volume 3 – Green - Centre fabric – Blue - Low volume 3

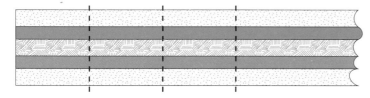

Fig 2.

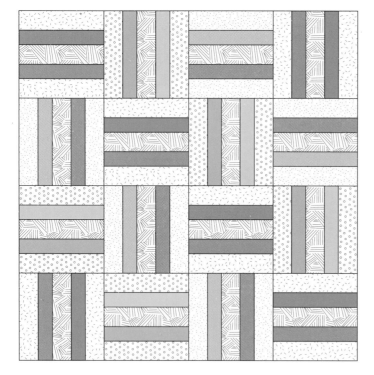

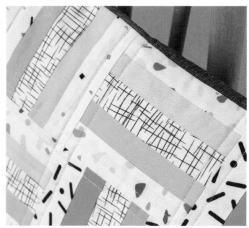

LAYOUT DIAGRAM

STEP 3 Cut each strip in to (x3) 4½" wide slices (Fig 2). You need a total of (x5) Green/Blue squares, (x5) Orange/Yellow squares and (x6) Red/Pink squares. You will have a few spare squares which you could use to play about with the layout.

STEP 4 Once you have the squares, arrange them in to rows following the layout diagram.

STEP 5 Sew the squares together into rows and then press the seams for rows 1 and 3 to the right and rows 2 and 4 to the left. Match the seams and sew the rows together so that you have a completed cushion top.

QUILTING YOUR CUSHION

STEP 6 Place the cushion top on to your piece of wadding and use spray baste or basting pins to keep steady. Optionally you may like to add a backing fabric under the wadding, this will keep the inner of your cushion nice and neat.

STEP 7 Quilt the cushion top in straight lines shadowing the squares. Once quilted trim back to 18½" square.

STEP 8 Hem a long straight edge on each of the cushion back pieces to hide the raw edges.

STEP 9 Use the envelope cushion tutorial to complete the cushion.

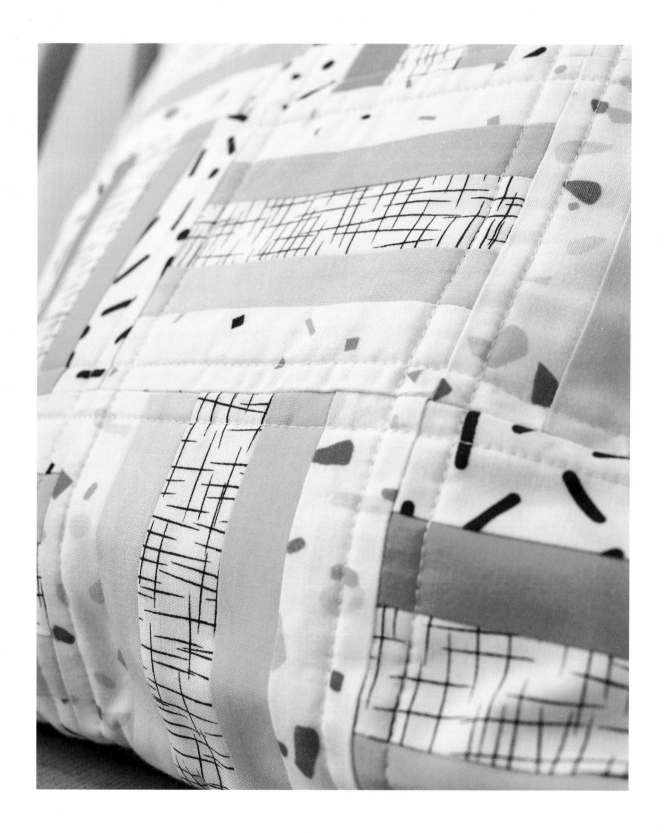

chapter five: mini projects

These three mini projects are nice and simple to create and are also great stash busters. I make lots as gifts for friends and family, and I love trying them out with different fabrics. I've kept to the rainbow theme and used quite a few bits of fabric that were left over from the larger projects found earlier in the book. The large rainbow star purse is one of my favourite projects to make and it's so handy to have around...

rainbow star purse

If you haven't already guessed, I love rainbows and stars! This large purse makes for a great supersized pencil case or makeup bag. I used waterproof fabric for the inner, which means you can wash it if your pens leak without ruining the outer fabric. You can use cotton as the inner fabric, if you have a favourite print.

Size: 12" x 10"

Fabric:

- ▨ (x1) 3¼" squares in each of Red, Orange, Yellow, Green, Green-Blue, Blue, Purple and Pink fabrics

- ▨ 1 F8 each of eight different Low volume fabrics

- ▨ 4½" black square

- ▨ (x1)14" (36cm) zip (can be trimmed if longer)

- ▨ 1 F8 purse backing fabric

- ▨ 1 FQ purse inner fabric

- ▨ 14" x 12" (36cm x 31cm wadding

CUTTING INSTRUCTIONS
From eight of the Low volume fabrics, cut;
(x3) 3¼" squares from each
From the remaining Low volume border fabric, cut;
(x2) 1½" x 12½" strips
From the purse backing fabric, cut;
(x1) 10½" x 12½" rectangle
From the purse inner fabrics, cut;
(x2) 10½" x 12½" rectangle

UNITS TO PREPARE
Half Square Triangles
The HSTs for this cushion are made using the two at a time HST method. To make the two HSTs, match together 3¼" squares in the following combinations:

STEP 1 Make the following HSTs in the following combinations:
(x1) Red / Low volume 1
(x1) Orange / Low volume 2
(x1) Yellow / Low volume 3
(x1) Green / Low volume 4
(x1) Green-Blue / Low volume 5
(x1) Blue / Low volume 6
(x1) Purple / Low volume 7
(x1) Pink / Low volume 8
(x12) Low volume / Low volume*

*mix up the Low volume fabrics in to six pairs to create the (x12) Low volume HSTs required.

STEP 2 Trim your HST units to 2 ½" (unfinished size)

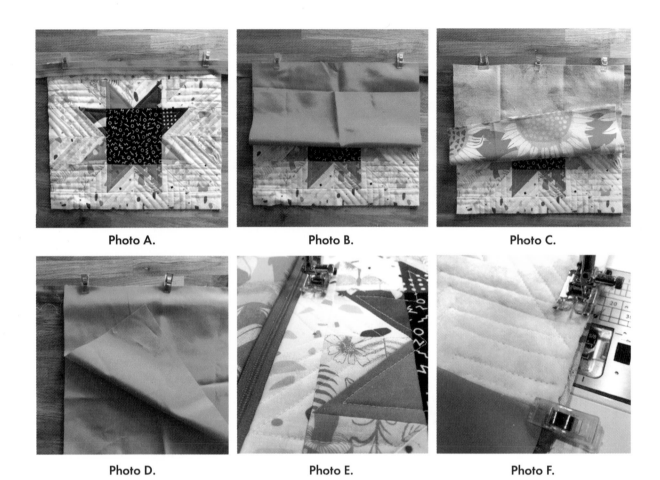

Photo A. Photo B. Photo C.

Photo D. Photo E. Photo F.

MAKING THE PURSE FRONT

STEP 3 Sew together the HSTs into the following pairs, creating a large Low volume V shape in the middle.

Blue-Green / Blue HST

Purple / Pink HST

Red / Orange HST

Yellow / Green HST

STEP 4 Sew the Green/Yellow HST pair to the left-hand side of the 4½" black square and the Purple/Pink HST pair to the right-hand side.

STEP 5 Sew a Low volume HST to each end of the Green-Blue / Blue HST pair and at each end of the Red/Orange HST pair.

STEP 6 Sew the Blue row to the top of the black square and the Orange row to the bottom of the black square.

STEP 7 make two rows of (x4) Low volume HSTs and add one row to each side of the star block.

STEP 8 Finish by adding a 12½" x 1½" Low volume border to the top and bottom.

STEP 9 Lay the purse front onto the wadding piece and then quilt the purse front. I chose to echo the star shape, with lines radiating outwards. Once quilted trim back to 10½" x 12½".

MAKING THE PURSE

STEP 10 Place the front of the purse (star) right side up on the work surface. Place the zip at the top of the purse front so that the top edges match up and

Photo G.

ensuring the zip teeth are facing down. (Photo A)

STEP 11 Place an inner fabric piece on top of the front and zip so that the right sides are facing together, and the top edges are matched up. (Photo B)

STEP 12 Clip or pin to hold the layers steady, then sew the zip in place by sewing through the three layers between the zip and the outer top edge.

STEP 13 Flip the layers so that the zip is at the top and the layers are now wrong sides together and right sides facing out.

STEP 14 Take the purse backing fabric and place it right side down on top of the front purse piece, ensuring the top edges of the fabrics and zip line up. (Photo C)

STEP 15 Turn over and then place the inner fabric on top of the attached inner piece, right sides together. Sew the zip in place as before. (Photo D)

STEP 16 Open up the sides so that the front is wrong sides together with an inner and the back is wrong sides together with an inner and the zip is aligned in the middle.

STEP 17 Topstitch a line approx. ¼" from where the zip meets the front fabric. As you are topstitching make sure that the inner fabric is nice and taut so that it doesn't get caught in the zip. Repeat the

topstitching on the back pieces. (Photo E)

STEP 18 Open the zip halfway and cut off the ends. Make sure the zip is open, so you don't cut off the zip pull.

STEP 19 Open up the purse and match the front and back fabrics so they are RST and the two inners are also RST. The zip will be in the middle, using a clip make sure that the zip teeth are facing down towards the inner fabric, this will help give you neat and tidy corners.

STEP 20 Sew along the left and right sides of the purse, making sure you take extra care as you sew over the zip. Place your hand inside the open outer fabrics and ensure the zip is correctly aligned and in an open position.

STEP 21 Once the zip is open you can sew up the bottom of the purse outers but leave bottom of the purse inners unsewn. (Photo F)

STEP 22 Clip the corners, then place your hand in the open (inner) end and pull the inner fabric through the zip. This turns the purse the inside out and you can now see your handy work again.

STEP 23 Give the corners a good poke and shape the purse, then either blind stitch or machine stitch the inner fabric in a matching cotton colour to finish the inside. (Photo G)

rainbow coasters

These rainbow coasters are a great little scrap busting project. You can use up all of your little scraps as long as they are 2¼" or larger. I used lots of the scraps I had left over from the other projects in this book, plus a few extras. This is a really simple project and a very quck make.

Size: 5 ½" square

Fabric:

- Scraps of various lengths in the seven rainbow colours
- 1 FQ Backing fabric
- 12" (31 cm) square wadding
- 1 FQ Binding fabric

PREPARING THE TOP

This is a great project for using up scraps by sewing them together into longer strips. These strips are then sewn to the wadding square.

STEP 1 On the 12" wadding square draw a line diagonally across the middle, then another line ¾" away from this line towards the left. Draw another line ¾" away, this time towards the right.

STEP 2 From these second lines, continue to draw lines diagonally at 1½" intervals. This will help with your fabric placement.

STEP 3 Gather together your scraps and create a pile for each of the seven colours used. Make sure that each scrap is at least 2¼" tall and vary in length from 1½" to 4".

STEP 4 Starting with Purple strip, sew together the Purple scraps so that you have a strip of fabric approximately 18" in length. Trim the strip so that it is 2" in height.

STEP 5 Create the same strips using the other six colours, in total you will need:

Red – (x1) 14" long strip & (x1) 5" long strip
Orange – (x1) 12" long strip & (x1) 8" long strip
Yellow – (x1) 8" long strip & (x1) 12" long strip
Green – (x1) 14" long strip
Blue – (x1) 16" long strip
Purple – (x1) 18" long strip
Pink – (x1) 16" long strip

STEP 6 Place the Purple 18" strip down so that the centre of the strip is on top of the centre diagonal line drawn on the wadding. (Fig 1)

STEP 7 Place the Pink 16" long strip RST with the Purple strip and the sew a ¼" seam along the top long raw edge. (Fig 2)

STEP 8 Fold over the Pink strip and iron flat. Take the 14" long Red strip

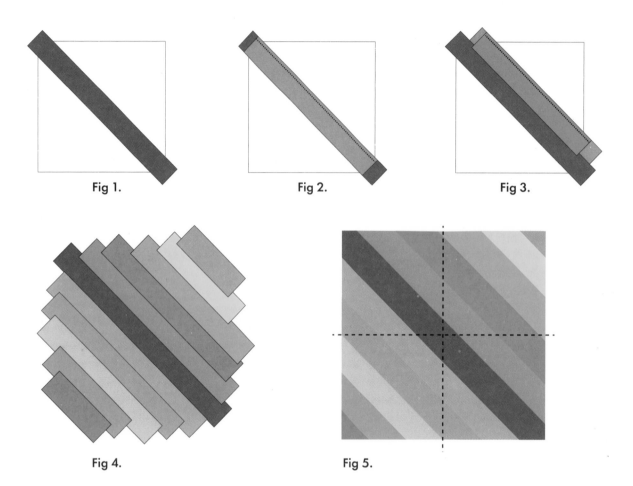

Fig 1.   Fig 2.   Fig 3.

Fig 4.   Fig 5.

and place RST together with the Pink strip so that the long raw edges are matched up. Sew together with a ¼" seam and then fold over the Pink strip and iron in place. (Fig 3)

STEP 9 Repeat with the Orange (12"), Yellow (8") and Green (5") strips until you reach the corner. Don't worry if there is a small gap at the corner as you are going to trim the wadding square.

STEP 10 Going back to the centre, line up the Blue (16") strip with the bottom diagonal edge of the Purple strip and then sew a ¼" seam along the bottom diagonal line.

STEP 11 Repeat with the Green (14"), Yellow (12"), Orange (8") and Red (5") strips until you reach the bottom corner. (Fig 4)

MAKING THE COASTERS

STEP 12 Place the backing fabric wrong side up in front of you and then place the front piece on top. Quilt the layers together. I quilted colour lines inside each striped piece.

STEP 13 Trim the quilted piece down to 11" square and then cut into four 5½" squares, (Fig 5) these are your coasters

STEP 14 Take the 2" binding strips and join them together to create one long piece. Fold the long binding strip in half lengthways. Cut the long binding strip into (x4) equal pieces, one for each coaster.

STEP 15 Attach the binding to the sides of the coasters in the same way you would bind a quilt and then hand stitch the binding on the back.

rainbow drawstring bag

The drawstring bag is a great little scrap buster. I searched through all of my off-cuts to find 2½" squares and the end result is a really striking, fun and practial design that is great for honing your cutting and sewing skills.

Size: 10" x 11"

Fabric:
- Scraps in rainbow colours, enough for (x50) 2 ½" squares
- 1 FQ for bag lining fabric
- 1 F8 Striped fabric
- 1 Yard cord

CUTTING INSTRUCTIONS
I used scrap 2½" squares in the following quantities for each colour:
(x6) Red
(x8) Orange
(x10) Yellow
(x8) Green
(x6) Green-Blue
(x4) Blue
(x4) Purple
(x4) Pink
From the striped fabric, cut;
(x2) 2" x 10" rectangles
From the bag inner fabric, cut;
(x2) 10 ½" squares

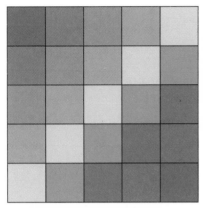

LAYOUT DIAGRAM

Photo A.

Photo B.

Photo C.

MAKING THE BAG

STEP 1 Sew the squares together by first sewing into rows and then joining the rows. Use the layout diagram as a guide. Make (x2) of these.

STEP 2 Take a 2" by 10" rectangle and fold the ends in by ¼" and then fold in by another ¼" to hide the raw edges. Top stitch the ends and then fold in half lengthways.

STEP 3 Place the front of the bag right side up and then place the top stitched rectangle in the middle at the top, so that the raw edges are aligned with the top of the bag front. (Photo A)

STEP 4 Place a bag inner RST with the front of the bag, clip or pin in place and sew together along the top with a ¼" seam. Repeat for back of the bag. (Photo B)

STEP 5 Open out the layers so that the lining fabric is at the top and the outer fabric is at the bottom and the striped casing is in the middle (Photo C)

STEP 6 Place the front piece and the back piece of the bags RST so that the outer pieces are matched, and the lining pieces are matched. Pin in place and then sew along the sides and the bottom of the outer piece. Leave the bottom of the inner piece open.

STEP 7 Pull the bag through the opening at the bottom and then close the inner fabric by folding in the raw edges and sewing shut.

STEP 8 Thread the ribbon/strap through the casing at the top to create the drawstring bag.

STEP 8 Thread the ribbon/strap through the casing at the top to create the drawstring bag.

shopping guide

Everyone has their favourite places to shop for fabric, right? There are so many amazing suppliers to choose from now, so here are a few of my mine. I've also included a list of the shops I buy my tools and products from...

Fabric shops (USA)

Pink Castle Fabrics
www.pinkcastlefabrics.com

Fat Quarter Shop
www.fatquartershop.com

Gather Here
www.gatherhereonline.com

Tools and products I use

Aurifil 50wt cotton thread
www.aurifil.com

Bloc-Loc Rulers
www.blocloc.com

Soak Flatter Spray
www.soakwash.com

Quilters Dream Batting
www.quiltersdreambatting.com

Fabric shops (UK)

Wool Warehouse
www.woolwarehouse.co.uk

The Fabric Fox
www.thefabricfox.co.uk

The Crafty Mastermind
www.thecraftymastermind.co.uk

The Eternal Maker
www.eternalmaker.com

Me and my fabric
www.meandmyfabric.com

Olive and Flo Handcraft
www.oliveandflohandcraft.co.uk

About the author

Paula Steel lives in in Lancashire with her husband and two cats. She started sewing again six years ago, when she finished her MBA and her daughter became a teenager. With a passion for colour, rainbows, geometrics and the 80s, and a-not-so-secret love of maths, Paula fell in love with quilting and hasn't looked back. Since leaving her former job in 2016, Paula now designs quilts for magazines, makes bespoke commissions and also works as a freelance technical quilt editor.

If you would like to see more of what Paula (or the cats!) are up to, check her out on Instagram at *@paulasteel.quilts*

Acknowledgements

This book was made a reality by the fantastic team at *White Owl Books* and Katherine Raderecht and her team of photographers and art directors. I also need to thank all the people who have helped me on my quilting journey by offering invaluable advice, encouragement and belief. The *Quilt Now* team gave me my first magazine commission piece and made me believe I could forge a career out of this. I also need to give a massive thank you to the lovely ladies at my local quilt group for testing patterns, editing my words, checking my maths! Special mentions also have to go to my 'binding fairy', Nichola, my 'quilting maths fairy', Sarah, and my 'wordsmith fairy', Debbie.